Braised Blue: Year One

Words By: Nicholas V. Nedin

Food By: Nicholas V. Nedin

Edited By: Robert Leigh Angus

Photography By: Nicholas V. Nedin

Interior Design By: Nicholas V. Nedin

Cover Art By: Mark Klein

Published By: Nicholas V. Nedin

To My Parents...
My most fervent supporters, roommates,
financiers, public relations team, sources of
inspiration, facilitators of unconditional love and
eaters of my mistakes.
I love you both and endless thanks.

A Very Special Thanks To:

Robert Leigh Angus of Octavia Press for putting this idea in my head, helping me navigate Amazon Create Space and editing my book.

Mark Klein for turning my stick figures and fragmented ideas into an awesome cover.

And last but not least my IndieGoGo Supporters: Laurie and Graham Fraser, Trevor and Jane (Future) Toombs, Marilynn Prettie and Brian Burchmore, Bruce and Mary Burchmore, Paula and Ed Bernard, Naomi Bernard, Ross and Sheri Scott, The Boys from Meat Club namely David Kidd, Jeremie and Shannon Jones, Lindsay Knudsen, David Greenaway, Bev and Bob Warner, Adam Verheyen, Julie Gibb and Christian Morrison, Chris Eder and Brian Peterson, Sarah Head, Dan Alvar, Julie Robinson and Jay Santarossa, Karlene Nielsen, Bryson "National" Parks

Table Of Contents:

Breakfast

Spring

Summer:

Autumn

Winter:

"*Opportunities to find deeper powers within ourselves come when life seems most challenging.*"
      - Joseph Campbell

My earliest memories were of food, sitting in my grandmothers house as she made all kinds of different Serbian dishes. It was simple food, peasant food, soul food (to steal a term from African American cuisine), it was not the extravagant ingredients that made this food special, it was the memories, the stories, the history and the love. This food was not dissimilar from anyone else's Balkan grandmother's food, what was different was the way she never measured anything, the seemingly haphazard dash of this and pinch of that which turned into magic at the end that captured me. It's the idea of wonder when someone cooks, the idea that you are creating something and that a group of ingredients can be elevated to something totally different and amazing that makes me want to cook. It's magic, it's alchemy, and it's something anyone can do.

Food is part of us, literally and figuratively, we eat to sustain and build our bodies but we also leave our imprint on food. Our history, as wide a culture and as narrow as a family is projected back onto the food we create, the wine we drink and the way we integrate food into our culture. We mark time with food, we mark events with food, and we pass food down to the next generation like we would an heirloom.

Braised Blue came from a dark place, a place of self-loathing, self-doubt and fear. I had never really put my words, my photography, or my food on display in such a public way. Words, Images, Food all swirling together being integrated, being changed becoming something different and hopefully amazing .I started Braised Blue after a bad break up and a few months on disability for a serious depression. A food blog had been something I had wanted to do for years but I focused on other endeavors. This time to reflect and recover allowed me to reevaluate what I was doing with my life and create a new path for myself.

But this book is about the year, the ebb and flow, the up and down.

Food has always been something that I loved to work with, a creative outlet among creative outlets. It wasn't until I read Kitchen Confidential while on a flight home from a week in Napa where I really began to understand that food and words were something that could be intertwined in a truly literary way. Anthony Bourdain's voice made me jealous, and inspired simultaneously. I think there is something in the way that Bourdain writes that infects the reader, his voice becomes part of your DNA. I feel like I have found my voice in this year and I hope that it now finds you.

I grew up in Amherstburg, Ontario a small commuter town south of Windsor on the southern tip of Canada. Essex County is a bountiful rural peninsula that afforded me a multitude of fresh produce growing up that I would have never gotten my hands on if I had grown up in a different place. I learned much about the liquor business. All of these places and experiences have shaped me, the blog and now this book.

What you are about to read is an experiment; it is not a cook book, it is not a memoir, it's also not a place for me to hock my photography or wax intellectual about food, wine and whiskey. This book is a year in the life of a blog, my blog, Braised Blue. It's a book that tries to make sense in print of a digital form that I don't think we've yet to really take advantage of when it comes to the world of food.

Thank you for picking up this book and I hope that it becomes something dog eared on your coffee table or kitchen shelf.

BREAKFAST:

The human brain is just a computer that would leave a puddle on your desk.

The brain is an organ that is just as chemical and electrical as it is biological tissue. We as human beings are where we are because of our brains. We can reason, we can problem solve and most importantly we can- based on past experience- predict the outcomes of our actions with relatively accuracy. But what happens when our brains don't do what we need them to do?

Anxiety is a natural physiological reaction to stress. We all deal with it, and most of us don't give it a second thought. But what if you were not able to turn off anxiety? What if taking a deep breath, having a glass of wine, or an orgasm wasn't enough to stem the tide of anxiety. What if it became so overwhelming that the fear of being anxious made you anxious?*

Over the past three years I have been dealing with an anxiety disorder that has at times been debilitating. For me, the anxiety that I experience will normally be followed by a depression. The more anxious I get, the more depressed I get. I like to think of it as a mood sling shot. The further I stretch myself the further away normal I will land. I am not going to list off many of my symptoms here because it's a cook book and many of them are not going to make you want to eat. They are physical and really not appetizing to talk about. **

Eating well is a huge part of dealing with anxiety and depression. Proteins, Carbs, fats, vitamins, and minerals all have major effects on the brain and the body. My first piece of advice is to eat breakfast. I spent years having coffee and maybe a muffin for breakfast. What I didn't know was that my caffeine and carb bomb was setting me up for failure, when it came to coping with my anxiety. Since getting my diet under control I make sure, I eat a good breakfast with lots of protein and a good amount of carbs. It sets me up for a great day. One breakfast I love is a few eggs, a couple pieces of toast and a whole avocado sliced up.

Avocado is a great fruit. It can add a creamy element to a dish without all the bad cholesterol and stomach ailments that comes from dairy. It gives dishes vibrant colour. Also avocados have tons of fibre and oleic acid which actually fools your endocrine system into feeling full sooner and longer.

Breakfast is a great base for your day. Whether you are battling depression and anxiety or you just want to be the best you can be today, a full stomach in the morning makes for a clear mind for the day.

*See every character Woody Allen has ever played.

**Here are the physical symptoms in a footnote do not read these if you are eating or planning on eating. Night sweats, hot flashes, nausea, stomach cramps, bloating, irritable bowel syndrome or colitis like lower gastro-intestinal symptoms, back spasms, headaches, tightness in the chest, hyper ventilation, vertigo, etc.

Recipe: Boozy French Toast w/ Tequila Blueberry Mascarpone Topping.

*And not just because serving children alcohol before school is a bad idea. It's heavy and totally unhealthy.

**A vanilla flavoured cognac…note to self do a piece on eau du vie sometime in the future. That should be good drunken fun.

*** The Topping should be fluffy in texture but also tart in flavour, between the tangy cheese, tequila, lemon zest and vinegar this should really be surprising flavour wise.

This is not your normal breakfast recipe this is not something you make for the kids before school.* It's more of one of those special occasion breakfasts where you want to impress someone. Possibly if you have friends visit or that first morning after a significant other sleeps over. This is one of those knock you on your ass, over the top breakfasts that you would feel horrible guilt about if you did it regularly.

Ingredients: 4 Thick Slices of Brioche

3 Eggs (beaten)

Navan**

1 tsp Cinnamon

2 cups- Mascarpone cheese (leave out for half an hour to bring the cheese to room temp.)

Lemon Zest

1 cup Blueberries

1/4 cup Balsamic vinegar

1/2 cup 100% Agave tequila blanco

Directions:

The Topping*: In a pot on low heat add butter, blueberries, tequila, and vinegar. Stir the mixture until the blueberries are soft and the liquid in the bottom of the pot has reduced by half. In a mixing bowl add your mascarpone and hand kneed it until it becomes soft and pliable. Add your blueberry, tequila, butter mixture and stir it in with the cheese. You don't want it to be uniform you want the blueberry and the reduction to almost marble the cheese. Then put the mixture in the fridge for 30 minutes.

The Toast: Beat your eggs into a wide bowl, mix in a few splashes of Navan. Dredge your brioche into the egg/booze mixture. Then dust the wet bread with the cinnamon. In a medium heat (oiled) pan, place the dredged bread. Ok really do I need to explain how to cook French toast? Like cook it and the outside of the bread gets kind of an egg crust on the outside. But seriously if you can't figure out when your French toast is done I am not sure why you are reading this.

Recipe: Huevos Rancheros

There is a song about beans being a magical fruit and their ability to produce prodigious flatulence. Now beyond the fact that beans are not a fruit, there is some magic that the people of Mexico have been able to work with beans that would blow your mind. Here is a breakfast recipe that is packed with protein, flavour and most importantly the magic of beans. I discovered Huevos Rancheros at a diner in Calgary who's name should be forgotten because their numerous health code violations should be how the public knows them. This is a simple Mexican dish popular in rural Mexico. Usually it consists of eggs, corn tortilla, refried beans, salsa, chilies, guacamole, and sour cream. But there is something magical that happens in the slurry of the beans, egg yolk, sour cream, and pork fat*. My version of this dish is a bit stripped down and a little more protein heavy and carb light.

*My version includes bacon and I assume pork fat falls from the sky in rural Mexico.

Ingredients:

4 strips of Bacon

4 Eggs

1 Can of Refried beans

Sour cream

Hot sauce (your choice)

Cilantro

Black pepper

Directions:

In a sauté pan (Pan 1) on medium heat put two pieces of bacon cooking until the fat is rendered and then to your level of doneness. In another pan (Pan 2) cook two strips of bacon again until the fat is rendered and the bacon is done to your preferred level of doneness. In Pan 1 cook your eggs in the bacon fat over easy. Please ensure the yolk is kept runny because the yolk is part of the magic of this dish. In pan 2 add your can of refried beans and possibly a little bit more bacon fat. You want the consistency of the beans to thin out a little but so the addition of a tiny bit of stock can help get the consistency of the beans to a level where it's not soupy but not chunky. This explanation of the consistency of the breakfast beans you are making seems much too long but seriously it vastly improves the overall deliciousness of the dish. When the beans are warm you want to plate up the beans beside the eggs so that you can easily break the yolks and mix them with the beans. Then top the beans with a healthy dollop of sour cream, a couple dashes of hot sauce and a sprig of cilantro more as an aromatic element. Try and get a composed bite of the yolk, the beans and the sour cream all in one.

Recipe: The Braised Blue Breakfast Burrito

The Breakfast Burrito is one of the most egregious culinary mistakes ever to grace the frozen food section of your gas station. Slimy eggs, rock hard imitation bacon, and radioactive hot cheese all turn a shitty flour tortilla into a soggy mine field of disappointment.

Today I am going to reinvent the breakfast burrito into something true to its roots and full of flavour.

Ingredients:

Corn tortilla

2 Eggs

1/2 cup Monterey jack cheese (grated)

Smoked bacon (thick sliced and cut into width wide strips)

1 Poblano chili (blistered on fire and cut into strips)

1 can Black beans (rinsed in cold water)

Cumin seed

Maple syrup

1 cup frozen Corn

1 Tomato (diced)

1 Red onion (finely diced)

1 Lime (juice)

1 Jalapeño (thin sliced)

Cilantro

Recipe Redux

"Wine for breakfast," you ask?
"Yes," I reply with an unimpressed look on my face.

"I've heard of champagne for breakfast but you're pairing a breakfast burrito with wine, that is crazy."

"So are your provincial views on wine and food, kojack." I open a bottle of dry, spicy Spanish rose.

"Is that wine pink?"

"You can leave now."

The above was a dramatization, speaking to the delicate nature of my relationship with my readers. Don't fucking doubt me, readers*, you can pair a dry Spanish rose with a breakfast burrito. The dry, but refreshing rose will work well with the spice of the dish and the acid will do well in cutting the fattiness of the bacon. It's a really great combination.

*I love you, but seriously don't doubt me or I will kick you out of my burrito and wine breakfast in bed.

*Maple Syrup adds such a great layer of flavour to this component of the dish.

**Sunny side up is too labour intensive and tricky for a dish with this many moving parts.

Directions:

The Beans: In a sauce pan render your bacon. Add your rinsed black beans, cumin seed, and blistered poblanos. Add a little maple syrup* and your frozen corn. Cook the beans for about 15 minutes until they begin to break down. Remove from heat and let sit.

The Salsa: In a bowl take your chopped tomato, onion, jalapeño, cumin seed and cilantro. Mix it all together and add 1/4 of a cup of fresh lime juice.(salt to taste)

The Eggs: I like to do my eggs over easy, because I like the yolks to run all over the dish and really mix in with everything. You can do scrambled eggs or whatever suits your fancy but I like the runny yolk.**

The Burrito: Take your corn tortilla and place it in an oiled pan for 30 seconds just to warm and toast the tortilla. Lay the burrito out and use your beans make a layer of beans. Then add your cheese, this will create a vein of melted cheese that runs through the burrito. Then on top of the cheese is the eggs, when the eggs are on, break the yolk and let it run into the beans and cheese. Finally top with the salsa and roll your burrito.

What do you call a thing that isn't an omelette and isn't a frittata but has elements of both? Well there is a place in Montreal called Cosmos Restaurant that does a dish called Mish Mash that will clog your arteries with joy*. The Cosmos Mish Mash was eggs, bacon, cheese, sausage, potato, tomato, ham, salami and half a loaf of bread worth of toast.

My version of Mish Mash is slightly less insane but it's by no means healthy. It is a great breakfast if you are going for a hike or need to stay full and energized for long periods of time. This recipe feeds two people.

Ingredients:

5 Eggs (Beaten)

5 strips Bacon** (cut into 1/4 inch pieces width wise)

2 Yukon Gold potatoes (shredded and soaked in water)

3 Green onions (cut very small)

1 tsp Fresh rosemary

1 cup Colby cheese (shredded)

Sour cream

Sriracha sauce.

Directions:

In a medium-hot oiled pan add your sliced bacon and render the fat. This should take a few minutes. Then add your potatoes, sautéing them in the bacon fat. As your potatoes begin to brown add your eggs and rosemary. As your eggs begin to set, skim off the uncooked eggs from the top and push them into the pan. Then add your shredded cheese and cook until melted. Once you plate this monstrosity add some sriracha sauce, a dollop of sour cream and top with green onions. Please make this only once a year and enjoy, I don't want my readers to suffer from heart disease.

*And cholesterol

**Thick cut and smoked bacon. Breakfast sausage or chorizo sausage works well also.

Recipe: Smoked Salmon, Spinach, Pine Nut and Rosemary Frittata

The frittata is an easy and rewarding dish that most people can make and most people have the ingredients for in their fridge. The recipe I am giving you is a little bit more exotic but you can substitute what I have here with any ingredients and it will turn out just as well.

What is great about a frittata is that in a single skillet you can feed three or four people or if you live alone it's something you can eat for any meal and it keeps for a few days in the fridge, so it's something you can eat for breakfast for three or four days. This is the perfect bachelor dish.

Recipe Redux: Drinking in the morning is something frowned upon by most people but pairing a sparkling wine, with breakfast, is hardly drinking. Think of it more as living. I would recommend a Cava from Spain. Cava is made by the same method as Champagne and costs about a quarter of the price. The bubbles are a perfect interplay between the fluffy egg and, the creamy crunchy pine nuts and the silky salmon. I would recommend Segura Viudas Reserva Heredad, at a twenty five dollar price point this dry cava will blow you away with it's quality and how it works perfectly with this dish. Plus it's a great example of how you can get champagne quality for a much lower price.

Ingredients:

8 Eggs (whisked in a bowl)

1 lb Smoked salmon

1/3 cup Pine nuts

Spinach

1 pinch of Rosemary

Fontina cheese (chunks)

Butter

Directions:

Preheat your oven safe pan(I prefer a cast iron skillet), to medium heat and add butter. Once the butter is melted add the pine nuts and toast them. This should take about 3 to 4 minutes. Then add the spinach. You want to just wilt the spinach in the butter and nuts until the green colour becomes more intense. Then add your eggs. You need to really whisk those eggs before they go in the pan. Whisking causes air to be infused into the egg. The more air you get into the egg the more fluffy they will turn out. You allow the bottom of the egg to set in the pan and then reduce the heat to low/medium and add your smoked salmon pieces. And cook for about two to three minutes. During this wait time, turn on the broiler on the oven. Once the frittata is mostly set there should be a layer of uncooked runny egg on top. Add your slices of fontina, rosemary, salt salnd pepper, and put the entire pan into the oven on the middle rack. Do not close the oven door and keep a close eye as the cheese melts and the top of the egg sets. Remove the pan from the oven, let the cheese firm back up for a few minutes and serve.

SPRING:

"You can cut all the flowers but you cannot keep Spring from coming."
-Pablo Neruda

I want my spring food to explode like a storm coming off Lake Erie.

Growing up in far Southern Ontario, I maybe didn't appreciate Spring as much as a should. I bet you thought I was going to talk about rebirth and regeneration but I'm not really going to do that. Spring to me is hot house tomatoes from Leamington, grey skies and ungodly amounts of slush. Spring meant stern looks from my mother for being too muddy from playing outside. In Amherstburg, Spring unfolds like a three act play. From slushy grey of late March and early April to the explosive storms of April and May to the sticky heat of June where we are lulled back to equilibrium.

My ideas of Spring food may be skewed by my geographic experience. Spring makes me think of the beginning of fresh produce, more delicate fare, vibrant colours and freshness. Rushing to grill your dinner as you feel the electricity in the air and the smell of a storm penetrating your nostrils as the sky sets to explode.

Pairing the big flavours of a Berkshire Pork Chop with the delicate texture of grilled zucchini, the nuttiness of Quinoa which has been infused with the spicy smoke of ancho peppers is spring to me. The integration of those fresh elements to something as comforting and traditional as a pork chop to me is Spring. Just as easily I could take the same pork chop pair it with a spiced apple sauce and root veggies and it becomes a Fall dish. It's those little tweaks in the way a dish is integrated that can bring a seasonal aspect to food.

The Grilled Ribeye with chimichurri is another example of this. A ribeye is great anytime of the year but bringing those big acidic and herbaceous flavours from the chimichurri and the intense green colour of the sauce punctuates and sets the dish in a time and place.

Spring is also about lightness, fresh clams with white wine sauce a pear coleslaw, crab cakes. There is a longing for a lightness when you get to Spring. Winter in Canada is long and heavy handed.

To me Spring is about reaching a critical mass and having it being energetically released. The long Winter of being cooped up indoors, the lack of sunlight, the monochromatic monotony. To translate that to food I find that spring food works best in flourishes of flavour, colour and aroma. Enjoy spring with me.

Recipe: Grilled Berkshire Pork Chop, w/ Grilled Zucchini and Ancho Quinoa Primavera

Berkshire Pork is as close to the platonic form of what pork should be as you will find. It's so good that I am going to show you how to make it work with a much healthier dish.

Ingredients:

Berkshire pork chops (bone in and frenched)

Salt

Pepper

1 large Zucchini (cut into strips)

1 Yellow pepper (diced)

3 Scallions (chopped)

1 dried Ancho chili

500ml Chicken stock*

1 cup Quinoa

Olive oil

Smoked paprika

Fresh parsley

Butter

*Most of the time you will see Quinoa recipes use water in the cooking process. Stock adds lots of flavour and some much needed fat to the grain.

Recipe Redux

Pork just screams for an intense wine. A California Zinfandel is a great pairing to match up with the saltiness of pork and the big flavours of this recipe. Ravenswood 2008 Old Hill Zinfandel is a great wine on it's own but with this recipe it really explodes with flavour. California Zin can be very high alcohol and the Old Hill comes in at 15% but the alcohol doesn't over power the rest of the components of the wine. It's nicely balanced and will be a crowd pleaser at your barbecue.

**There will be those who do listen to this and then go back to this footnote and are browbeaten. I told you not to overcook the damn pork chop but you did anyway. You're better than that.

Directions:

The Pork Chop:

I like to treat a Berkshire Chop simply. Brush on some olive oil, and then coarse sea salt and pepper. More or less what I would do with a steak. You will want the flavour of the meat on display. I grill the meat on high heat to render and crisp the capsule of fat that wraps the cut, just like a steak to medium rare. I like my pork with a little bit of pink. I know that this is not everyone's cup of tea, so please cook it however you want it. Just remember that pork can dry out fast.**

The Zucchini:

Get a mixing bowl and cover the strips with olive oil, salt, pepper, and smoked paprika. I am a huge fan of having some smokey flavours to pair with a pork dish. You then put the zucchini on the grill just long enough to get some nice score marks and to blister the skin. Normally about 3 minutes per side.

The Ancho Quinoa Primavera:

Get a medium sized sauce pan. 250 ML of quinoa, 500ML of chicken stock and a broken up dried ancho chili. Cook on medium/high for about 15 minutes, until the quinoa begins to get translucent and begin to unravel. Then add about 1/8 of a stick of butter, along with the yellow pepper and scallion for about 2 or three minutes. The quinoa should reduce to a risotto type texture. You then take the sauce pan off the heat and cover for five minutes to let the starches reconstitute.

Plating: I am a fan of putting the pork chop on top of the quinoa. This helps really integrate the spicy smokiness of the ancho flavoured quinoa and the meat. The zucchini also echoes the smokiness with the smoked paprika notes. I also like some fresh parsley to just give the dish some nice fresh lift with all the salty and smoky going on.

Veal Involtini is one of my favourite dishes in my repertoire because it is simple and quick to make, it always tastes great and you can use pretty much any kind of fresh seasonal ingredients to punctuate the dish. Normally I would do this dish with a simple side salad but i leave that up to you. Pasta works, as well as risotto, but that all depends on how heavy you want the meal to be. Involtini is kind of a "choose your own flavour" profile and go with it dish. I love this particular flavour profile because fennel bulb produces such a subtle anise flavour which still seems to shine through the asparagus and the cheese, as well as the sauce. But it's never overpoweringly fennel-ey. And the textures that come into play in the involtini is really great. If you like simple light summer fare this is a perfect dish. Also, I am teaching you how to make a homemade red sauce from scratch in 15 minutes. So you can stop buying the junk in the bottle.

The Involtini

Ingredients:

4 pieces of Veal Scallopini (top round)*

4 Slices of Prosciutto

1 Fennel Bulb (diced)

4 Pieces of Asparagus

1 cup of Pecorino Romano cheese (grated)

2 tbs of Lemon Thyme.

Directions: Take your pounded out veal and salt the meat. Lay the meat out and begin to assemble the filling of the involtini. First line the veal with the prosciutto then at one end place your asparagus, fennel, cheese and thyme. The hard part is getting the right amount of filling so that you can roll a nice neat meat burrito** type contraption. Use toothpicks to hold the involtini together. Do that another three times. This may take you a few tries to master so just be patient. Then on a medium heated and oiled barbecue grill, put the involtini on and grill until the meat has been cooked through and the filling begins to ooze out. Do not grill too hot as any connective tissue in the veal will begin to warm the pounded out meat and it may become tough.

*The veal should be pounded out to be about 1/8 of an inch thick. To pound the veal put it between two pieces of Saran Wrap and pound with the flat side of a meat hammer or use a rolling pin, until the desired thickness is reached.

**Not my word. Mario Batali calls Involtini a meat burrito. Which brings up mental images that you will have seared into your brain for years.

The Sauce

Ingredients:

1 Large Can of Diced Tomatoes.

3 tbs Olive Oil

2 Cloves of Garlic (smashed)

1 Onion Chopped

2 Serrano Chilis (finely chopped with about 1/3 of the seeds left in)

1 Leaf of Sage

Directions: In a sauce pan add olive oil, onions and salt. Sweat onions until translucent. Add your garlic and cook down for 2-3 minutes. Add your chilis and cook those down. Then add your tomatoes and sage leaf. Stir everything together. And simmer for about fifteen minutes, stirring every few minutes to make sure nothing it sticking.

Putting it together:

This is not tough. Get your involtini (or involtino if you only want to have one) and cover it with the sauce. Make a quick herb salad with a vinaigrette and some nice bread to sop up the spicy sauce with. This is a great casual dish for a summer out on the patio.

Recipe Redux

This dish opens you up to many different wines depending on the flavour profile you are playing with. One interesting pairing with this dish is a Chilean Carmenere. Carmenere is a heavy bodied red grape varietial that has its roots in Bordeaux but has become Chile's signature grape varital. With deep dark notes of cocoa, and leather, and bright berry fruit this wine works really well to bring out the flavours of asparagus and the sauce. One tip with a Carmenere is that it needs time to open up. So try opening your bottle about 45 minutes before drinking. This will get rid of a pungent green pepper note that can overpower the wine. Some oxidization will erase that unpleasant note and really bring out the great things about this varietal.

Foods You Should Know: Steak

Today is my birthday so I decided to talk about what I would choose as my birthday meal nine times out of ten. What makes a good steak is a very personal thing. The cut, the heat, the seasoning - all of these things are important when purchasing and preparing your favourite steak. I personally like a Boneless Ribeye, seasoned with black pepper, sea salt and finished with Fleur De Sel*, cooked blue. When you read this know I am assuming you have a barbecue as pan frying a steak is a whole other monster which I may release as a recipe one day.

Before You Buy:

If you are going to the butcher ask them questions. Where did the animal come from? How many days did you age it? How did you age it? The things you want to hear is that the animal is local(less time to market) The meat has been aged for 21 to 28 days, and that is has been dry aged. Most super market steaks have been wet aged in vacuum bags. It takes less time to age but it makes the meat usually less marbled with fat and less flavourful.

The Cuts: There are dozens of different cuts of beef that are considered steaks. They are regional and they go by lots of different names. I will give you a few that you will find at your local butcher shop.**

The Strip-loin: Also known as the New York Strip this is a medium lean steak with a very dense texture with a thick fat/connective tissue cap on one side. Super tender if seared properly and cooked at lower heat, needs to be cooked with the fat cap on to lock in the juices.

The Ribeye: Also known as a prime rib steak. A good cut has tons of fat marbled through it. The texture is much less dense than a strip loin. One of the most flavourful cuts of steak. It should be well seared and then taken off the grill. Overcooking a ribeye is a crime against humanity.

The Porterhouse: Also known as the T-Bone. This is a combination cut of the strip loin and the tenderloin. It's usually very expensive because of the sheer size of the cut. I personally dislike it, because it is wasteful, difficult to eat and it never cooks evenly enough for my liking.

The Fillet Mignon: The Fillet Mignon is cut from the small end of the tenderloin. It's a very expensive cut and is so tender most steak lovers actually dislike it. It also doesn't have a ton of natural flavour so it just screams for a béarnaise sauce or some kind of exotic rub with some flavour. Nothing like spending 30 bucks for steaks and having to slather them in cream sauce or wrap them in bacon to make them taste good.

The Sirloin: The Sirloin steak is a less expensive cut of steak which is very flavourful and ranges from very lean to nicely marbled. It's a bit inconsistent when it comes to quality but it's wonderful cut up for a steak sandwich or a salad.

The Flank Steak: The most utilitarian cut. It's a long, thin cut of beef. It has lots of connective tissue which can be problematic if it's over cooked. But all kinds of great dishes like The London Broil use flank steak. The beef is super flavourful and quite reasonably priced.

The Heats

Raw: This is not usually something reserved for steaks. Sashimi, carpaccio, and tartare are just a few raw beef applications.

Blue: Seared on the outside and raw on the inside. My rule of thumb is 3 minutes on a screaming hot grill on each side. Score it, make it look pretty and take it off the grill. Of course this varies and you need to use your judgement.

Rare: Seared on the outside and with a little more cooking than Blue. The interior of the steak should be ruby red, fading to pink and then to the sear on the outside.

Medium Rare: Almost cooked totally through. Just a bit of red in the middle but mostly pink fading into the sear.

Medium: Cooked through but still a little bit of colour in the middle of the steak. No pink, but lots of juice.

Well: Cooked through, usually with a good char on the outside. Not my cup of tea but a lot of people fear the pink.

Seasoning:

I am a minimalist when it comes to steak, I like to buy more expensive cuts and let the meat do the talking. I prep it with olive oil, black pepper and sea salt. This allows the steak to get a nice caramelized crust with lots of flavour. With some of the lesser steak cuts, I love to do a spice rub, there are lots of fantastic ones out there that range from Montreal Style with sea salt, coriander, and black pepper, to southwestern with a selection of dried chilies, cumin and sugar. Sometimes life happens, and you have to get a grocery store steak and work some magic with a marinade (I like teriyaki with a little bourbon, for this because it really does well to break down connective tissue). If you don't have a barbecue first I am sorry and second doing a pan fried steak in a nice cast iron skillet can be magical with the right rub and technique.

Like I said earlier in the article, steak is a personal thing. Everyone has their right to be absolutely wrong about how they like their steak.***

*Fleur De Sel is a hand harvested sea salt from Brittany, France. It has a much higher mineral content than most other salts and an uneven texture which gives a slight crunch on the outside of your meat.

**Yah, notice I didn't say super market, or grocery store? Butchering is more and more becoming a lost art.

***Cooking a great cut of meat to well done seems like a crime to me, as does slathering a steak in BBQ sauce. That is just wrong.

As you may have read in the previous article on steak, I love ribeye steaks. I have always been a advocate of the simplicity of a steak but there are exceptions to this. Sometimes a chimichurri is a great condiment for a steak. A chimichurri is a South American sauce that is normally used to top grilled meat. A blend of parsley, oil, vinegar, garlic, cloves, and chilies, chimichurri provides a great companion to steak because it bring bright acidity, fresh herbal notes and spice which do wonders in giving a fresh accent to the steak.

The Steak

Ingredients: 2 Ribeye steaks

Sea salt

Black pepper

Olive oil

Directions: Rub the steaks with the olive oil and then season liberally with the salt and pepper. Then on a very hot grill, sear both sides and cook to your preferred heat. I am a rare kind of guy (or even blue if the steak is nice enough) but cook it as incorrectly as you feel you should cook it.

The Chimichurri

Ingredients: 1.5 cups Fresh parsley

2 tbs Mexican oregano

3 Cloves of garlic (finely diced)

1/2 cup Olive oil

2 tbs of Red wine vinegar

1 tsp Sea salt

1 tsp Black pepper

1 tsp Crushed D'abola chilies

Recipe Redux

This dish is a very simple blend of big meaty flavours coming together with bright acidity and herbaceousness. The wine that I would choose for this dish would need to be able to stand up to the steak while also having some ability to highlight what makes the Chimichurri so great. My choice is a Chilean wine I think I may have talked about on this blog before but in the name of not checking through a couple dozen wine articles I will just pretend that I didn't. Causino Macul Finis Terrae, is a wonderful wine from one of the oldest vineyards in Chile. It's a blend of Cabernet, Merlot and Syrah which makes for a wonderfully balanced red with enough backbone to stand up to the steak but all kinds of complexity that will work well in highlighting the herbs and the acid of the chimichurri.

Directions: Put the parsley and oregano into a food processor with the garlic, oil, salt and spices and pulse the processor a few times to make a minced sauce. Then spoon out into a bowl and add the vinegar and stir. Serve at room temperature with your steak.

In Vino Veritas: 5 Wines For Your Cellar

The Every Day Drinker: This should be a bottle of wine that doesn't break the bank. For me, I like to spend between 15 to 18 dollars on something from the Old World. I've found that you rarely can match the bang for your buck you get from Portugal, Spain and Italy. You can find some fantastic wines from Abruzzo in central Italy for 12 to 15 dollars that will give twenty dollar wines from the New World a run for their money. The region of Terras Do Sado from Portugal makes some fantastic Touriqua Nacional that come in around 18 dollars.

The Dinner Party Star: You should always have a good bottle of wine to bring with you to a dinner party. Now not all dinner parties are created equal. A rep once told me there is friend wine and then there is brother in law wine. For friend wine think red, think approachable, think versatile, and spend ten to fifteen dollars more than you would spend on an every day drinker ($25-$30). This is a wine that makes a statement but doesn't go over anyone's head. An Aussie Shiraz from The Coonawarra, a Chilean Cabernet or Merlot from Maipo or Colchagua. These are wines that are familiar but deliver huge quality for a reasonable price.

The Mind Blower: Sometimes you need to drink something that makes you reevaluate the wines you love. There are two Italian varietals that I love to drink just as a way for me to reconsider what wine should be, Nebbiolo and Nero D'Avola. One wine native to the far north of the county one native to Sicily. Nebbiolo is a noble grape of Piedmonte. Its name is derived from the italian word "nebbia" which means fog or cloud. Nebbiolo is harvested late in the growing season usually when thick fogs invade the mountainous growing regions. But there is a deeper meaning to this as well, Nebbiolo as a wine is also like a fog, shapeless, mysterious, without form. The Nebbiolo grape is used in the production of three famous Piedmontese wines Barolo, Barberesco and Gattinara. These wines can run you a pretty penny, and need some pretty serious aging but they may change your life.

Nero D'avola is a grape native to Sicly, its name literally means "black of Avola". The wine is an inky purple colour and can taste sweet and jammy, like an Aussie shiraz or tannic and complex. If I am going to stump my friends at a tasting Nero D'Avola is my go to wine. Wine geeks can never place it, and rarely dislike it. It's a great way to make yourself look like the smartest wine drinker in the room.

The Patio Wine: Most people would assume I hate white wine. And that is somewhat true, I hate bad white wine. Bad red wine is something I can choke down with food, but bad white wine isn't something I can deal with. But there is a time and a place for a white. Sitting on a patio or a deck on a hot day is such an occasion. For those days I look to France

Out of France, I love a Chablis, I want that flinty, minerality and austere flavour profile. It's refreshing, it's bone dry and it's acidity fools my mouth into thinking it's cold even when it warms up a little bit.

The Celebratory Bottle: Now you are probably thinking Champagne. Sure, you can drop ungodly amounts of cash on a bottle of Champagne. I would rather buy some sparkling wine from Limoux from the southwestern part of France. You can get great bottles of bubbly for 1/3 of the price of Champagne. I personally don't need to have bubbly to celebrate. I would rather open a really special red. Whether it be a California cult wine, a Super Tuscan from Bolgheri or a Bordeaux, celebration does not mean bubbles to me. Drink what you like when you are celebrating.

The world of wine is almost endless. Every bottle has a story, and a history. The more we drink hopefully the more we learn about the world.

Foods You Should Know: Oysters

Oysters are a divisive food. Either you love them or they make your skin crawl. But what if I was to tell you that they are one of Canada's greatest fishery resources? Canada farms some of the best Oysters in the world, and this is great for those of us who love Oysters. We get them fresh, and we get lots of different varieties from all over Canada.

But we also have a problem. Even though Canadian waters produce large quantities of high quality oysters, Canadian companies rarely control these stocks. Recently, on the west coast The Fanny Bay Oysters were bought out by a larger American company Taylor Shellfish. The Fanny Bay Oyster Company represented the last Canadian owned and operated oyster farm on the West coast. We as Canadians are becoming less and less involved with this great resource and down the road it may become less available to us.

Now for those who really don't care about Oysters and think they are snot on a shell. Who cares who owns and runs Canadian fisheries? You should, because the more the people and the government of Canada doesn't support its food producers the less control we have over what is being produced, how it's being produced and where the food on our table comes from. We all have a vested interest in supporting Canadian food producers.

*"He was a bold man that first ate an oyster"- Jonathan Swift

Now I am not going to try to sell anyone that they should or should not eat raw oysters. They do take a modicum of bravery to eat as Swift noted*. If you've ever had the misfortune of eating a bad oyster the violence of the illness that comes with it could turn you off for life. I've been there and I totally understand, vomiting until your eyes go blood shot for a week is never fun, but you go back to alcohol right?

**Squid, Cuttlefish, Octopi, and snails are just four of the 85,000 different species of Mollusks.

Oysters come from the Mollusk Phylum.** Oysters are what are known as Bivalves which also include muscles and clams. Oysters do grow in the wild but what humans eat are farmed. As to allow for easy harvesting and to protect fragile seafloor ecosystems. They are by nature a green crop, they cannot survive in pollution, they remove carbon dioxide from the ocean in their shell production process, and they create natural habitats for fish.

Oysters are known as a great aphrodisiac. They have high levels of zinc, vitamin E and dopamine, which can help battle depression and help get your date into the sack. They also go great with wine, beer and whiskey. Charles Dickens spoke about "oysters and stout," as the working man's lunch in Victorian Britain. In A Moveable Feast Hemingway talked about his love of oysters and dry white wine.

Oysters also don't need to be raw. Oysters Rockefeller is a classic New Orleans dish that combines a puree of green vegetables, bread crumbs, spices and butter to a oyster on the half shell. It is rich and spectacularly tasty. I will eventually release my baked oyster recipe, which contains bacon, smoked gouda and other fun stuff. Deep fried oysters are great in a sandwich or as a finger food with a nice dipping sauce.So don't fear the oyster. Embrace their salty, sweet, slimy shelled friend and expand your food horizons.

Nothing makes me feel like more of a Kennedy than a bowl of New England Clam Chowder.* It's rich, it's creamy, and it makes me incredibly sick. I am lactose intolerant and I am still willing to take the pain every so often. But there is hope. I made a dish last week that I had never made before. It was a take a southern Italian Clams in white wine sauce. And you now get to make it too.

This is a relatively easy dish in that it's hard to screw up as long as you keep an eye on things. There are two separate preparations in this dish. First is the creation of a Clam Stock. Second is the creation of the actual clam sauce. The stock is the key for some great flavour in the sauce.

The Stock

Ingredients:

Recipe Redux: This is an easy one. I would go with, M. Chapoutier La Ciboiseis a Cotes Du Rhone blend from Luberon. This blend of Grenache Blanc, Vermentino, Ugni Blanc, and Roussanne, which gives you a great soft white with stone fruit notes, citrus and minerality. It works really nicely with the clams and the broth. I would recommend not chilling this wine down too much. Refrigerate remove from fridge, and before serving wait about 15 minutes.

12 Little neck clams**

2 Tbs Sea salt

2 Sage leaves

Enough Water to Cover The Clams In The Pot

1 Cup Dry acidic white wine. (Trebbiano)

Before you do anything wash your clams and scrub them with some kind of brush or sponge. This will get any grit off the outside of the clams. Then place the clams in a pot with sea salt, cover the clams in hot water and white wine. Put the pot on high heat and bring to a boil. Keep the boil for about four minutes. This will open the clams and release any grit that is inside of them. Remove the clams and reduce heat, add the sage leaves.   Pour the broth through a strainer, to catch any large pieces of shell that may be in the liquid, into a large container. Leave the container for 15 minutes. Any grit will settle to the bottom. Do not stir this or move it, if possible.

*Wait till the audio book comes out and I do this recipe in my John Kennedy voice. "Ask not what you're clam broth can do for you."

**I like little neck clams because they have a nice dense meat that is a little bit sweeter than their older brothers.

The Sauce

Ingredients:

1 Red onion (finely chopped)

1 clove Garlic (smashed and chopped fine.)

1/2 Cup of White wine.

Olive Oil

2 Roma tomatoes (diced)

Clams (left over from the broth)***

1 Tbs Smoked paprika

1 Container of Clam stock

Sage (from the stock)

Directions:

Sweat the onions and garlic in olive oil in a sauce pan. Add the tomato and increase the heat on the sauce pan.   Add the paprika. Let the mixture reduce a bit and then add a quarter cup of wine. Let the wine reduce by half and add the rest of the wine and a ladle of stock to deglaze. Reduce heat to a simmer for 15 minutes. Taste the sauce and add salt as needed. At this point you add your clams back into the sauce. You will let these simmer in the sauce for about two minutes just to reheat. Since you have already cooked your clams, you only need to heat them up again and allow them to take on the flavour of the sauce. Serve.

What the hell am I going to do with this?

You are going to pour it over rice, quinoa or couscous. Or you are going to cook some linguini or another large gauge pasta that is going to hold the sauce. Now you should toss the pasta in the sauce for about a minute, and serve.****

*** You will want to take the clams out of their shells. Wash them to ensure no grit remains and leave whole.

****Pouring sauce over cooked already plated pasta is a sin. As is rinsing the pasta after it's cooked. If you are going to have something starchy and bad for you, do it right.

Foods You Should Know: The PoBoy Sandwich

New Orleans, summer, 1929. A transit strike slows the city to a halt. A former transit worker named Benny Martin, in support of his former colleagues offers a free sandwich made of deep fried kitchen scraps. During this four month strike, the jobless workers from all over the city flock to Martin's restaurant. The staff begins to call these men Poor Boys, which of course with the NOLA accent quickly becomes PO'Boys. Hence forth the Po'Boy Sandwich is born.*

In keeping with New Orleans' character the Po'Boy becomes a staple item on every menu in town. And in true New Orleans spirit the Po'Boy becomes elevated to a different level. No longer kitchen scraps on day old bread, the Po'boy has gone artisan. The classic Po'By has fried shrimp or oysters, usually with a garlic aioli or red eye gravy painted onto a baguette. It's simple, it's fast, it's delicious when done correctly.

I personally like a Po'Boy with fried Oysters, smoked bacon, arugula, and a garlic spread on the bread. I have also tried a Vietnamese Po'Boy that had Shrimp, with Asian slaw and hot sauce which I loved long time.* I have also seen Po'Boys with white fish or perch.

So I put it to my readers, find me a place in the Windsor area, that will make me a Po'Boy with local ingredients. And if that doesn't exist somebody put that on your menu, I will be at the front of the line for one.

Sorry Asia

**The social history of food, and wine for that matter, almost always has an element of peasant food being elevated and becoming "gourmet". This is an example of this elevation happening within the last 80 years.*

The Angel's Share: The Other Whiskey From the Other Island

I've noticed in the past 24 hours an influx of visitors to Braised Blue from Ireland*. I had been holding back this article because I wanted to wait for St. Patrick's day to release an article about Irish Whiskey as a response to the need people have to drink crappy green beer and break into the "incase of St. Patrick's day" box that resides under their beds*. But because I fear a potato with a note tied to it being thrown through my window tonight saying, "Wattabout Our Whis-key fucka", I decided to do this today and save myself the clean up job.

The first legal distillery in the United Kingdom was not a Scotch Whisky distillery it was actually in Ireland. In 1608 Bushmills distillery opened and for the first time, legally, continued a tradition of distilling that began with Irish monks as early as 500-600 AD. These monks travelled Europe and learned much more than just their faith, they learned to distill. Now back in this time distillation wasn't really for drinking purposes, alcohol is to this day a big part of perfume. And because the middle ages were also a time in history where bathing was frowned upon. Perfumery was a valuable business for the monks to learn. But sometimes you just need to drink some perfume and somehow these monks figured out their distilled grain matter was also a great medicinal cure for not being able to touch women.** So Uisce Beatha was born, translated to "water of life" this grain spirit was probably quite potent but also not so good for you, but a small amount of it could do what a gallon of beer could do.

Now there are some fundamental difference between Irish Whiskey and Scotch Whisky beyond the addition of an E in the Irish spelling. First is an obvious one, Irish whiskey must be distilled and aged in Ireland. Second is the aging time for Irish Whiskey is 3 years as compared to the Scottish standard of four years, and though it's not a law, traditionally Irish Whiskey is distilled three times vs. the Scottish tradition of two times distillation.*** Generally the flavour of Irish Whiskey is lighter and the nose is a bit more fruit driven. With the exception of Connemara, Irish Whiskies are unpeated and the kilning process is done with coal or natural gas.

There are three major distilleries in Ireland. The Bushmills Distillery, The Cooley Distillery and The New Midleton Distillery. The Bushmills Distillery clearly produces Bushmills Irish Whiskey. The Cooley Distillery produces such wonderful brands as Kilbeggan, Tyrconnell, and Connemara. And finally Jameson the biggest brand of Irish Whiskey in the world is produced at the New Midleton Distillery along with Tullimore Dew, Powers, Paddy's, Red Breast and Green Spot. Sadly there are almost no independent distillers of Irish Whiskey that can be found in Canada.

Irish Whisky also comes in a few different classifications:

Blended Irish Whisky: Is produced in a continuous still and can be blends from all different distilleries on Ireland. Generally it only spends the minimum three years in oak and gets a healthy dose of spirit caramel. ex Jameson's, Bushmills, Black Bush, Paddy's Tullimore Dew

Single Pot Stilled: These are batch distilled in a pot still and generally see between 8-15 years of age. ex Jameson's 15 Pot Still, Redbreast, Green Spot

Single Malt Irish Whiskey: Made from 100% Barley Malt and comes from one distillery. Just like Scottish Single Malt: Bushmills 10,12,16, Connemara, Tyrconnell

Single Grain Irish Whiskey: Made from a single strain of wheat. Greenore 8,10,12,18

In all Ireland has a great distilling tradition and some really beautiful whiskies which in many cases are more approachable than Scotch Whisky. Jameson's 12 was my entry point into Scotch, and I love the simple, but subtle flavours that Irish Whisky provides. If you want to get into Scotch but the powerful spirits have deterred you maybe trying Irish Whiskey will give you a kickstart.

*Sorry Ireland but prepare for some slights about your height, alcoholism, penchant for getting into fights, your translucent skin, the potato famine, James Joyce, U2, Leprechauns, catholic guilt, catholic shame, Catholicism, protestant guilt, protestant shame, gingers, freckles, and jigs. Also imagine me tearing up a photo of the pope.

**This box contains:

1 Deep Blue Sea CD that makes you proclaim "look I am kind if Irishish."

1 "Kiss me I'm Irish" t-shirt you got at Old Navy in 2nd year university.

1 Stupid hat, obnoxious visor, pair of green goggles, or Moosehead foam antlers

1 Blinking LED light that clips to your shirt or hangs around your neck in shot-glass form

***Sorry Catholics.

****There are exceptions to these traditions which I have laid out in other articles so settle down whiskey nerds.

Foods You Should Know: The Five Mother Sauces

Think of the five mother sauces as the bosses of crime families. These mother sauces have their own very distinct technique but these techniques and recipes can be tweaked to make other sauces. If Hollandaise sauce was a crime family* that a Béarnaise sauce would be the underboss of the Hollandaise sauce family. Before we get started there are two things that most of these sauces need before you can start. Either a Roux or a Stock or both. A roux is a thickening agent in three of the mother sauces. It's basically flour and fat** simmered until they have been integrated. Depending on how long you cook the roux the colour will be different ranging from white to black. A stock is a flavoured water preparation made from meat, vegetables, bones etc.

Béchamel Sauce:

Also known as a white sauce, milk, flour and butter are all you need to make a basic béchamel sauce, but normally onions, herbs and nutmeg are incorporated. Béchamel should be quite thick and can be used in many different applications usually in baked pastas.

Some of the other classic sauces which are based off of the Béchamel are the Mornay Sauce which is made with cheese. Nantua Sauce which is made with shellfish, butter and cream. Creme Sauce which is made with heavy cream. Mustard Sauce which is made with mustard seeds.

What you should make with a béchamel based sauce? Try something easy. Make your own macaroni and cheese. Create a mornay sauce and use that as your cheese sauce for the macaroni for a super rich and delicious version of Kraft Dinner.

Veloute Sauce:

A veloute is one of the oldest of the mother sauces. It starts with a chicken/veal/fish stock which is thickened with a white roux it has much less thickness than a béchamel sauce. Veloute sauce is a great all purpose starter for soups.

Some other classic sauces based on the veloute are Allemande sauce which adds egg yolks, heavy cream and lemon juice. The Normandy sauce which adds fish and oyster stock and mushrooms. Hungarian sauce which adds onions, paprika and white wine. And the sauce vin blanc also known as White Wine sauce.

What you should make with a veloute? Making a great chicken pot pie with a veloute sauce is a great way to pack a bunch of flavour into a classic comfort food dish.

Espagnole Sauce:

Also known as a brown sauce an espagnole sauce is very similar to the veloute in that it's a mixture of a brown stock*** and a roux, but it also adds tomato paste and mirepoix***. What comes out is a flavourful sauce which can be used in many applications and this sauce can be made into a demi-glaze by adding an equal part brown stock and reducing by half. Some other classic sauces which are derived from espagnole are: Marchand du Vin Sauce (aka red wine reduction) which adds red wine and is reduced by half. The Lyonnaise which added onions fried in butter. The Robert sauce which add shallots, white wine, butter and mustard seed. The Chasseur sauce which add mushrooms, white wine, shallow and tomato confiture.

Hollandaise Sauce:

Hollandaise sauce is the most distinct of the mother sauces in it's preparation and it's flavour. The other sauces use roux and stock but hollandaise is an emulsification of clarified butter and egg yolk. Flavour wise the sauce is buttery and tangy. As a note on the safety of hollandaise based sauces, the use of clarified butter is very tricky as it needs to be simmered at a low heat which can be a potent breeding ground for bacteria. I tend to not trust hollandaise sauce at restaurants because it is very easy to neglect and e-coli is not fun.

The classic sauces that derivate from hollandaise are: Béarnaise sauce, which adds tarragon and chervil with either a meat glaze or a tomato glaze. Maltaise sauce which adds blood orange. Noisette which add brown butter. Bravaroise adds a reduction of peppers, horseradish, thyme, bay leaf, vinegar and crayfish.

What can you make with hollandaise sauce? Béarnaise sauce is an amazing addition to a steak. It really matches well with the big meat flavours which are contrasted by the tanginess and herbal quality of the sauce.

Tomato Sauce:

This is much like a tomato sauce you would use on your pasta but it is much more complex in flavour and a little tougher to make. Tomato sauce uses salted pork for a stock base as well as a hambone with tomatoes and other aromatic veggies.**** The sauce will be sweet but savory as well, and it will be thicker than your normal pasta sauce.

Some other classic sauces that derivate from tomato sauce are: Provençal sauce which adds mushrooms, sugar, garlic, parsley and oil. Portugaise which adds fried onions, tomato concasse, meat glaze, garlic and parsley. Meat sauce which adds ground or chunked meat to the tomato sauce

What can you do with a tomato sauce? Put it on your pasta. It's much more intense and flavourful than the crap you get out of a can or bottle. It takes about 30 minutes to make and it's beautiful stuff.

---

*The Hollandaise Crime Family is known for their human trafficking but at expanding into the illegal importation of clarified butter.

**Normally butter

***Brown stock comes from the roasted bones of beef or veal. It is a much richer stock than chicken.

****Mirepoix is a combination of onions, celery and carrots which can be added to a stock to add flavour. You can either strain the mirepoix or add the mixture wrapped in a cheese cloth.

*****Onion, garlic, shallot

Pot luck dinners with your co-workers are a trap. They seem like a great idea when you are discussing a staff social in a meeting, but they are a festival to twice heated, over cooked yuck. I find large groups of people difficult to handle with my anxiety. It is actually a common trigger for many people with anxiety disorders. As a rule I would avoid them at all costs, but if you cannot avoid having to attend I have an action plan for you.

1. Volunteer to Prepare an H'orderve: You have already won, you food will be eaten first while people haven't had their stomach filled with greasy chicken wings, or the dreaded vegetarian lasagna that always gets raved about by only the women who over eagerly volunteers to make on every occasion.*

2. Show Up To the Party Early: You know you don't want to stay and hear about how well your co-workers kids are doing, at in their advanced play course, after they have had their strawberry margarita. You get in early under the guise of getting your h'orderve heated, and then you bail out early, before the human resource department starts trying to make people feel included.

3. Help Out the Host: You need to have a solid conversation with the host, who will remember how sweet you were for the next few years, after you help them with a few set up tasks. Yah that's right, I am telling you to go to a party to do work. This work will pay off in spades when the host defends your surly attitude with the girls from accounts payable and your early exit.

4. Make This Recipe: It's easy, it tastes amazing, and when you make something good you will look like a brooding food genius and not the twitchy person who keeps eye-fucking the exit.

*No man, gay or straight, has ever produced a vegetarian lasagna that he would ever think to unleash on the world. We are secretly a prideful gender. Also as a general rule for everyone in the world. Your no-bake cheese cake sucks, it has always sucked and it will always suck. It's SOOOOOOOO easy and it tastes like a lie with a graham cracker crust.

Recipe Redux: This is such a great appetizer which works well with all kinds of crisp white wines. But here is an idea, try it with some bubbly. I recommend Antech Blanquette De Limoux. Everyone knows Champagne, but sparkling wine is produced in a few other places in France. Limoux is a region in the south of France. Their sparking wines are lively, with floral noses and great minerality and super fine bubbles. There will be a delicate interplay between the wine, the cheese and the thinly sliced meat. Think of the pairing is more of a textural pairing than flavours.

Ingredients: 1 Stick fresh french bread.

4 Shallots (medium chop)

1/4 cup Salted butter

1 tbs Red chili flakes

1 tbs Brown sugar

Canola oil

1 lb. of Serrano ham (shaved)**

10 pearls of Bocconcini

Sea salt

Directions(Phase 1): Start by sweating the shallots in the
canola oil at medium low hear. Keep the shallots moving
because they are more delicate than onion. They also
caramelize faster than onions, but we are going to take a
caramelization short cut*** because you don't love these
people you are cooking for. When the onions are sweated add
your red pepper flakes, butter, and brown sugar. Continue to
cook this mixture until the shallots brown. This should take
5 or 6 minutes. You then pour the contents of the pan through
a strainer into a bowl. This will separate your shallots and
the sweet and spicy shallot butter you are going to butter
your French beard with.

Grab your ham and get pieces of the meat that are about the
size of the palm of your hand. Place small amount of the
shallots in the middle of the ham and wrap it up into a
little shalloty ham parcel. Do 20 of these.

Cut the French stick about 3/4 of an inch thick. You should
get about 20 pieces out of your run of the mill French stick.
By now the compound butter will have started to harden.
Spread the butter onto the bread and then place your ham and
onion ball onto the bread. Put them on a baking sheet and
cover with foil. Bring your container of Bocconcini with you.

Directions(Phase 2): Once you get to your location remove the
foil. Cut your pearls of Bocconcini in half and place the
cheese on top of the pouch of ham and shallot. Then sprinkle
with sea salt. Put the oven on broil, let it heat up and
insert baking sheet and watch until the cheese has melted.
Then pass them around like that project manager at least

** Serrano Ham is
similar to
Prosciutto but
it's from Spain,
it has a little
more smokiness and
it's usually a
little cheaper.

*** Caramelization
is a little tricky
with shallots you
really need to pay
attention and give
a crap. Adding
some brown sugar
will kick the
caramelization
process into gear
as soon as the
shallots are
sweated and a 35
minute task
becomes a 15
minute task.

Foods You Should Know: Parmigiano Reggiano

I haven't talked much about cheese on this blog and that is a problem. So when current events are brought to my attention*, I must jump at the chance of a teachable moment. On May 20th of this year an earthquake hit the northern Italian region of Emilia Romagna**, destroying about two billion euros worth of its key export Parmigiano Reggiano or to the lay person Parmasean Cheese. Large aging houses for Italy's best known cheese were rocked by the quake and years worth of product was destroyed. This means most likely sky high prices and shortages of the cheese.

Italy is serious about food and wine. So serious in fact that they have created systems of regionality and quality control to make sure that producers stick to the highest standards while at the same time protecting producers against competition from outside their region. This DOC system for cheese, wine, vinegar, olive oil, etc, allows producers to make their products using traditional methods, and ingredients while using more modern supply chain and exportation tactics.

What is it and how is it made?

Parmigiano Reggiano is a cows milk cheese. I am not going to go into the entire process of how the cheese is made because it is really complicated and exhaustive but I will try and do a quick summery. Raw whole milk is blended with skimmed milk to create a partly skimmed milk. That mixture is added to copper vats which are used to heat and cool the mixture***, whey starter and rennet is added. Once the milk curdles the curd is collected and the wheels of cheese are then produced. It normally takes around 115 lbs. of curd to create one wheel of cheese. The cheese is then pressed into that wheel shape and then stamped and labelled as DOC Parmigiano Reggiano. The aging process then begins. The cheese is taken for brining(salt water) and aged for about 25 days. After the brining process the cheese is dry aged for a minimum of 12 months. After 12 months the cheese is tested and graded by the government run DOC inspection agent. Cheese with lower grades are then readied for the market and high graded cheeses are left to age longer.

Why is Parmigiano Reggiano so good?

Parmigiano Reggiano is great because it is one of the rare examples of Umami in non Asian food. Umami is the fifth distinct taste that we were never taught in school(Sweet, Sour, Salty, Bitter, Umami). Umami is a savory, or deep brothy flavour which is prevalent in soy products which usually reside in asian cuisine. We now know that in hard, salty, aged cheese Umami is also very present. This flavour, whether we recognize it or not, makes our brains stop and say, "oh shit, I like that." It's also why Parmigiano Reggiano is such a good condiment, you can put it on anything, just like Soy Sauce is to asian cuisine.

So what does this Earthquake mean to me?

We you can look at in two ways. First, this is the end of the world, I am going to end up paying half my salary for the thing I love and that sucks. Or second, is Parmigiano Reggiano is too expensive maybe I can expand my horizons and see what other kinds of cheeses I can use as a substitute. I have two of these substitutes for you right now.

1. Peccorino Romano: A sheep's milk cheese made on the island of Sardinia*** from sheep which are raised in Lazio****. It has many of the same flavour qualities as Parmigiano Reggiano but it costs less and for those with Lactose issues is lactose free. It's a great replacement for Parmigiano Reggiano.

2. Manchego Viejo: Spain's answer to Parmigiano Reggiano. Its actually an aged sheep's milk cheese which goes through a different process which includes a wax coating and olive oil baths. It comes from the region of La Mancha and it's younger versions are very different than it's aged version which is harder and saltier.

So now that you know a little more about Parmigiano Reggiano, and the current problems with its production. Go to your local cheese shop and buy it while it's still a reasonable price, it lasts a long time and if you buy enough you could end up being the neighbourhood hook up for all things Umami.

*Thanks to reader and all around cutie Sarah L for the link to this earthquake story.

**Beyond amazing food, wine and cheese, Emilia Romagna also produces great filmmakers. Bernardo Bertolucci, Michelangelo Antonioni and Fredrico Fellini are all from the northern Italian province. *Trying not to make a Last Tango In Paris Butter joke.

***Copper is an amazing metal in many ways. It is very conductive when it comes to heating and cooling but it also has the ability to bind to many impurities in food and spirits. Which actually means that your milk will have fewer, heavy metals, free radicals and radioactivity when copper is used in it's production.

****Sardinia is an island in the Mediterranean near Corsica. It's an Italian territory but it is very much it's own distinct region.

*****Lazio is the central Italian province and Rome is the capital.

Recipe: Herbed Flat Bread w/ Prosciutto, Caramelized Onions & Figs

I love pizza and I can make pizza but I have a problem with eating too much pizza so something quelling that pizza craving with something pizza like while making something that is a little bit more portion controlled. This flat bread recipe is also great at an appetizer or hors d'oeuvre. You can choose to make your own dough but I am not normally much for baking but there is pre made pizza doughs that you can pick up at a lot of grocery stores. They do really well because all you need to do is portion out your flatbreads, wake the dough up with a little flour and water, and then kneed in your herbs. But I digress on talking about the inter-workings of the recipe before the recipe begins. The pre recipe preamble is what differentiates Braised Blue from other food blog where people slide in boring anecdotes about what their kids like to eat. But what can I say about pizza? It's awesome, who doesn't like pizza?*

Ingredients:

1 pre-made Pizza dough (about the size of my fist.**)

1/2 cup Basil (fresh chopped)

1/4 cup Oregano (fresh chopped)

1 Onion (rough chopped

5 Figs (quartered)

5 Slices prosciutto (thin sliced)

1 Roma tomato (diced)

1 tbs Dried red chilies

Goat cheese

Olive oil

Sea salt

Black pepper

* Nazis, The Khmer Rouge, The Gluten Intolerant?

**Guess I am going to have to create some kind of fist size exemplar if I am going to continue to compare things to my fists.

Directions:

Take your dough and kneed your chopped herbs into it with some salt and pepper. Stretch the dough into a rough rectangle and put it onto a cookie sheet that has a thin layer of corn meal on it which will keep the crust from sticking while at the same time allowing the crust to crisp. In an oiled pan on medium heat add your onions and cook them down until they begin to brown and release their sugar. Add your figs to the pan and continue to sauté with the onions. The sugars from the figs should kind of kick start the caramelization of the onions. One the onions and figs have really released their sugar take them off the heat. Then top the pizza with the onion fig preparation it should act almost as a sauce it should be sticky and sweet add the chili flakes tomatoes and prosciutto. Then add some chunks of goat cheese to your liking. I like just a little bit of goat cheese but by all means slather the damn thing in goaty goodness. In an oven heated to 425 degrees and cook the pizza until the crust turns golden brown and the toppings begin to really melt together and integrate. It should take about 12 minutes but it really depends on your oven. Enjoy!

About this size. Also here is a lesson you should all learn. Never, ever google search the word "fist" because it's a rabbit hole that you really don't want to get lost in.

Foods You Should Know: Polenta

Polenta is one of the most interesting and delicious ingredients you've probably never tried. It's an incredibly simple ingredient that can be used in numerous ways. Polenta is ground corn meal that is cooking into a paste.

Polenta is a Latin word, meaning hulled which refers to the process of crushing grain. In Europe corn was not grown until the 16th century, before that dating back to Roman times polenta was made from crushed ferro, millet, chick peas or spelt. It was a slave food more commonly known as gruel or porridge.

When Europeans began to produce polenta with corn, they found that the starch in corn made the texture of the usually unappetizing dish, velvety smooth, and the slightly sweet neutral flavour of corn was a perfect canvas for the infusion of flavour. Different ingredients started being used with the usually plain staple food. Cheeses, butter and lard were used to add fat content and really kick the flavour in the dish up a notch.

Up until recently polenta was categorized as peasant food, usually served as a thick mash potato like consistency, flavoured with anchovy or other salted fish. Its use has now expanded to becoming a rich flavourful staple of those who love rustic Italian comfort food.

Polenta isn't just a porridge like substance, much like grits. Once you make polenta you can leave it to set and it will congeal into a solid substance which can be used in many different applications. In Friuli, in northern Italy, polenta is left to set and then cut into discs and then fried or baked. This creates almost like a corn meal chip or fritter, which adds a great crunch to a dish.

You can buy ready made polenta from your grocery store or Italian specialty store in long tubes which look like tube of cookie dough*. There are already prepared polenta that you can either boil down into it's creamy form or cut into different shapes and sizes for other cooking preparations. One of my favourites is to cut the polenta into cubes and toss with a butter, garlic, and parmigiano reggiano.** It's a great gluten free alternative to pasta and is pre cooked so all you need to do it cut it up into the size you want and then just add it to any dish that normally calls for pasta.

What makes polenta so great is that you're only limited to the chef's imagination. It's a blank canvas that can take so many great forms and flavours. The next time you are at the grocery store pick some up and see what you can create.

*Do your best not to mistake polenta for cookie dough when you are up late and possibly of bended mind. It won't be so pleasant.

**I have actually tried a polenta that was infused with cream, sugar and fruit and used as the filling in a Napoleon. It was a really great idea for added some substance and staying power to a pastry application when it has to stand up to warm weather.

Recipe: Cornmeal Crab Cakes w/ Horseradish Aioli

After a conversation last night with a friend I remembered that I had a pretty awesome crab cake recipe in my back pocket. So let me put on my regulation Bobby Flay Boston accent and we will get cooking.

This recipe only will yield four medium sized crab cakes so if you want to do more, double the recipe.

The Crab Cakes

Ingredients:

1 Egg (beaten)

2 tbs Cornmeal

4 tbs Bread crumbs

2 cloves of Garlic (finely chopped)

1 tsp Fresh thyme

2 Serrano chilies (finely chopped)

1/2 cup of Sour cream

1.5 tbs of Grainy mustard

6 ounces of Crab meat*

Flour as needed

Directions: In a mixing bowl add everything but the cornmeal. Fold everything in together until you have a nice consistent mixture that you can form cakes out of. If the mixture is too loose add flour to help it all bind. Then refrigerate for 6 hours, this will allow the flavours to marry. Form four medium sized crab cakes and dredge them in the cornmeal, make sure you really get a nice coating of cornmeal on the cakes. In an oiled cast iron skillet on medium high heat place the cakes into the hot oil. I would do two at a time, crowding the pan will not allow a nice crust to form. My rule of thumb is about 4-6 minutes on each side of the cake, but use your judgement, you want the outside to be crisp and the inside to be hot but still moist.

*You can either use canned crab or cook your own crab meat. It all depends on whether or not you have fresh crab at your disposal. Canned will do in a pinch.

The Aioli

Ingredients:

2 Egg Yolks

1 tbs white wine vinegar

1 tbs salt

1 tbs brown sugar

1 cup olive oil

3 tbs of horseradish grated

2 cloves of garlic minced

Directions:

Add all the ingredients to a food processor** and blend until the mixture is whipped into a uniform mayonnaise or aioli consistency.

Serve the crab cakes topped with a small dollop of aioli. The spice of the cake and the horseradish in the aioli will work really well together with the sweetness of the crab and the crunchiness of the cornmeal coating. Enjoy.

**You can hand whisk an aioli but because I assume you, the reader, is lazy, the food processor does just as well.

Recipe Redux: Crab cakes are an interestingly tricky thing to pair with wine. You want something with nice acidity to give a lift to the palette because this is an appetizer, but you also want to compliment the texture of the cakes with something that has some body. My choice would be a Macon Village from Burgundy in France. This Chardonnay is a great blend of acidic minerality, light fruit, floral notes, and a nutty quality. This mouth filling but relatively light flavoured style of wine will do wonders with the crab cakes.

The Angel's Share: Coming To America

When I started The Angel's Share as a feature I didn't mean for it to only be about scotch. It was a Whisky feature and today's article is about Bourbon. Bourbon is America's answer to Scotch. A product of a time, place and people, bourbon really owes its existence to the South, most notably the state of Kentucky.

Origins

The beginnings of bourbon are not as clear as you would think something that is only a couple hundred years old should be but it is no less interesting. There are multiple claims and stories that take credit for the invention of bourbon. Some say the Baptist Minister Elijah Craig first invented the drink by placing moonshine into charred oak barrels creating a brick red coloured substance. Jacob Spears also gets credit for inventing bourbon though his legend suffers for lack of preaching. The reality is that much like any food or drink invention there was many people who were doing similar things because they were limited to only a few choices of what to make their hooch out of. In Eastern Kentucky, corn was plentiful, the water was very pure and there was a healthy population of Scottish, Irish and Welch immigrants who had grown up distilling.

The Bourbon Laws

There were a series of laws passed in 1964 by the United States government to protect bourbon from foreign counterfeits and the degradation of the quality of the product.

First, to be labeled Bourbon or Straight Bourbon on the label the whiskey must be made in the United States of America.

Second, the whiskey must be produced from at least 51% corn mash.

Third, the whiskey must be aged in new oak barrels that have been charred.*

Fourth, the distillate must not exceed 160 proof (80%).

Fifth, the distillate must not be put into barrels at the proof higher than 125 proof (62.5%)

Sixth, the whiskey must be bottled at no less than 80 proof (40%).

Seventh, the whiskey must be aged for a minimum of two years, and have no colouring or flavouring added .

There are also laws when it comes to labeling as bourbon comes in two varieties, Straight Bourbon and Small Batch Bourbon. Straight Bourbon denotes the following of the bourbon laws and small batch bourbon denotes the blending process in which a blender chooses the finest straight bourbons to create a much higher quality product.

Now knowing these laws I will debunk a couple of common myths and misconceptions.

1) *"Jack Daniels is technically a Bourbon even though it doesn't follow the Bourbon Laws because it's so popular."* Wrong on so many levels but with a small glimmer of truth. First the truth, when NAFTA was ratified the word Bourbon was used as a legal blanket word for all American Whiskies. So yes in the wording of a law that has nothing to do with alcohol, distillation or consumer protection, Jack Daniels can be described as a Bourbon. Now the Myth, Jack Daniels is not considered a bourbon because they use a charcoal mellowing process before bottling. This is a process that Jack Daniels patented himself and it gives JD a distinct flavour and mouth feel.

2) *"Bourbon can only come from Bourbon County in Kentucky."* As you read above Bourbon can be made anywhere in the United States. If the Hawaiians wanted to make a Maui Wowui Bourbon they, by law, could. Also Bourbon County now does not contain a single distillery, the once huge county has been broken into over 20 smaller counties many of the distilleries you know fall within the old Bourbon County area but not in the current Bourbon County.

What Does Braised Blue Recommend?

There are dozens of bourbons out there and they all have very distinct styles and flavour profiles. I love Bookers but its smokiness and harsh alcohol content is usual off putting to the beginner. A seasoned veteran should also have a bottle of Maker's Mark because it's great for mixing or drinking straight up. And bang for your buck wise, Jim Beam seven year old will blow your mind for under $30.   I will give you three bourbons to try. All three are drastically different and distinct but trying them will kind of give you are idea of the flavour profiles you can run across with when it comes to bourbon.

1. Buffalo Trace: A bourbon that will show you what bourbon is all about. Rich, spicy, full of flavours of dried fruit, vanilla and and English toffee, this whiskey isn't mellow. It comes at you with a punch but then the richness lingers on your palette forever. Not many whiskies have a finish like Buffalo Trace.

2. Basil Hayden's: The most mellow bourbon I've ever had. From the Jim Beam small batch line, Basil Hayden's offers a high rye content (which normally adds to spicy character in a bourbon) but is balanced by an 8 year aging. This pale straw yellow coloured whiskey will lull you into drinking it neat and then before you know it you are glued to your easy chair.

3.Wild Turkey Rare Breed: Wild Turkey has a reputation of being harsh and that reputation is 100% founded. The Rare Breed is a blend of 6, 8 and 12 year old offerings of Wild Turkey and what you get is one of the most intensely satisfying bourbons known to man. Hints of citrus, mint, caramel, and pipe tobacco on the nose bely the rich palette of Christmas spice, candied pecan, hot chilies and freshly baked bread. It sounds strange but this red leather coloured bourbon will blow your mind.

* Kind of a cool thing about the use of New Oak Barrels. Cooperage(barrel making) is one of the most difficult disciplines in carpentry. When the Bourbon Laws were created there was a deal struck between Bourbon producers and the Coopers Union to protect first the jobs of coopers as well as the trade its self. Oak Barrels can be reused, but these laws make the producers go to the extra expense of producing thousands of new barrels. I think it's pretty refreshing that this practice is still part of the tradition of bourbon production.(Also the Scotch industry would be in big trouble if there wasn't thousands of used bourbon barrels to purchase every year.)

Recipe: Asian Pear Coleslaw

I had an intense coleslaw conversation on Friday night which turned into the creation below. There were intense stances taken against cream based coleslaws and then racial lines were drawn between Asia and Europe. Salad has always been a non-starter in my experience but the topic of coleslaw seems to divide*.

Ingredients:

1 Asian pear (julienned)

1 cup Red cabbage (shredded)

1 Carrot (shredded)

1 cup Cashews (slivered)

1/2 cup Rice wine vinegar

1 tbs Aged balsamic vinegar

1/2 cup Canola oil

1 sprig Cilantro

Directions: In a bowl add all of your ingredients (except the cashews) hand toss everything together, cover with plastic wrap and refrigerated over night. Toss the salad a few more times over the course of the evening just to allow the dressing to really marry with the vegetables. When serving add your slivered cashews and enjoy.**

*Naomi Bernard has strong feelings about the topic of Coleslaw.

**I also though topping the salad some crunchy tempura for a nice texture would be a great idea. But I totally forgot to

Foods You Should Know: Chorizo Sausage

In this blog I have used Chorizo Sausage in a bunch of different applications. So I figured I would enlighten those who had no idea what I was talking about and at the same time go over some of the varieties of Chorizo you may be able to find at your local farmers market.

Chorizo Sausage is a pork sausage that has its origins in Spain and Portugal. It is actually a generic term that encompasses sausage from a few different areas of the Iberian Peninsula.

Chorizos can be prepared in two ways. Either as a fresh sausage that can be cooked on its own or used in various cooking applications or as a cured sausage which can be eaten without cooking. Both preparations have the same base ingredients, coarsely ground pork meat and fat, smoked red peppers, smoked paprika, wine and other spices. All of this good stuff is mixed together and allowed to marry. Then the sausage is put into its casings. The fresh are sent off to market and the cured are smoked and as well as fermentation process is usually applied. What you get is a salty, spicy, and savory blend of flavours that works well with many different cuisines.

Chorizo Sausage isn't only made in Europe. Mexico has their own spicy take on the famous sausage. Instead of the coarsely ground pork of Europe, Mexican Chorizo finely minces the meat. Instead of smoked red peppers and paprika the Mexicans substitute chili peppers, cilantro, and garlic. Regionally you get even more variation in Mexico. In the regions of Toluca you get a Green Chorizo which adds tomatillo and cilantro. In other areas, bitter mexican chocolate is used.

There are also South American takes on the Chorizo that get even weirder. Beef actually becomes the main meat used in South America. In Brazil, chorizo refers not to pork meat but blood sausage*. Cinnamon, nutmeg, whole peppercorns are all used in south america as substitutes for the expensive and difficult to attain smoked paprika.

The Chorizo Sausage in any of its forms is a great substitute for beef in a sauce**, a fantastic breakfast meat and just an overall great thing to throw on the grill and blow a few friends minds with. As you have seen in many of my past recipes it's a great way to put a different spin on an old tired recipe.

*Blood Sausage is exactly what it sounds like. A sausage with pork meat from various areas of the pig as well as the blood from the pig. It creates a strongly flavourful sausage.

**As you will see in a few recipes later on in this book. Keep those peepers open.

SUMMER:

"Eighth grade's a distant rumor, a tabled issue...freed to an unspoiled summer, that inviting medium for doodling in self-transformation. "
-Jonathan Lethem

My Summer food is to be made with a drink in your hand and friends in tow.

We are conditioned growing up that summer is a time of respite. Respite from school, respite from the winter, respite from responsibility. A time to wipe the slate clean and live more authentically.

I grew up with sticky hot summers. Unrelenting humidity and heat that makes breathing a chore on some days. Food was cooked out doors on a grill, drinks were plentiful. Clouds rolling by in the backyard as flames kiss food and glasses sweat almost as much as those holding them.

Summer food to me is more about variety, the roadside stands in Essex County are working in full force, everything is fresh, everything is at your fingertips and it's all about those simple fresh items on a plate.

There is also a lightness to summer cuisine. Whether it's a cedar plank smoked salmon, fish tacos or a great summer salad there is so much to taste, so much to enjoy and so many great things to drink.

I love just allowing an ingredient to speak for itself any time of the year but the summer, when things are at their freshest, I find this is infinitely more true.

My summer food is also about sharing. It's about standing around the grill and shooting the shit with your friends, enjoying a burger from the grill or meat being transformed in a cocoon of smoke to something infinitely more complex and flavorful.

It's about quiet dinners with a significant other over a bottle of wine as the sun over the Detroit River sets in Technicolor. It's about an ice cold cocktail, a quiet moment with a book and the sun beating down on you in a moment of solitude.

Let's tip one (or five) to summer.

Drinks You Should Know: The Caesar

Today I am hungover. Not horribly hungover, but I have felt better. Hangovers have many remedies but one such remedy has become a Canadian way of life, The Caesar.

A savory cocktail made with vodka, Clamato juice, Worcestershire sauce, and a variety of spices, the Caesar was invented in Calgary, Alberta in 1969. Walter Chell, manager of the Calgary Inn, created the drink, and it took off in popularity.

Though there is no official edict, it is generally accepted that the Caesar is the official cocktail of Canada. The internet also tells me that the city of Calgary on May 13th 2009, celebrated the 40th anniversary of the Caesar by making it Caesar Day. I was in Calgary for this occasion and must have missed it.*

Caesars are typically made with vodka, but there have been many variations created over time. I personally like my Caesar with gin, though I've seen recipes that include Canadian whisky, beer, and different flavoured vodka.

The garnish is another big part of the Caesar. Usually the glass is rimmed with celery salt, a stick of celery is placed in the glass and a lime is used to garnish. Different establishments will usually change this part of the drink. Pickled Green Beans, cucumbers and asparagus are also common replacements for the exceeding yawn worthy celery. I would be remised to not make a joke about eating a pickle while getting pickled.

Many people enjoy a Caesar with spice. Hot sauce is a common addition to a Caesar, but pickled hot peppers, horseradish and wasabi are all interesting and sinus clearing ways to put a different twist on the drink.

Caesars of course are touted for their restorative powers when in the throws of a hangover. Part of this is because a hangover is partially caused by a withdrawal from alcohol and a Caesar evens out those symptoms**. The drink it's self is pretty healthy as far as cocktails go. It has lots of vitamins from the tomato, protein from the clam broth, and electrolytes from the salt.***

So tonight (or tomorrow morning) when you want to pour yourself a drink, do yourself a favour and mix a Caesar.

*I was probably stuck in traffic.

**I am not promoting morning drinking to cure the DTs, but sometimes a caesar isn't a bad idea if you need to feel better for a morning golf game.

***I should have titled this piece, "Braised Blue becomes a bad influence and grasps as straws while making health claims about a vodka based cocktail."

Recipe: The Braised Blue Burger

I love a good burger, and I cook a good burger. But what goes into a great burger? I mean there is a large part of the population who couldn't give a shit about the burger they are eating, right? MacDonald's is still turning out their mush burgers, by the billions. Burger King is still carpet bombing their burgers with mayonnaise like there was some kind of insurgent, allergic to eggs hiding in the lettuce. People even go to chain restaurants like Kelsey's and pay 10 dollars to have a burger that has been blessed with bacon and cheese. Well I give a shit about my burger, and soon, you will as well.

So first I need to explain the elements of this burger that I am not making from scratch. First is the bun. Go to your local bakery (not your local supermarket) and get whatever kind of buns your little heart desires. I like an onion bun with some poppy seeds for texture. You also need condiments. I like to take good old Heinz Ketchup and mix it with Sriracha sauce and mayonnaise*. I also like to use pickles on my burger for some acidity. I like to use aged cheddar and triple cream brie cheese.

Ingredients: 500 g Medium ground beef chuck

500 g Medium ground beef brisket

1 egg (beaten)

1 onion (grated)

2 cloves Garlic (grated)

1 cup Bread crumbs (finely blended in a food processor)

1 tbs Worcestershire sauce

Salt

Pepper

6 sprigs Rosemary (finely chopped)**

Tomatoes (sliced)

Arugula

4 pieces of Pea meal bacon

4 Eggs

*Some people call this Asian Ketchup but I prefer Vietnamese Vaseline, or Nummy Napalm.

**Beef cooked on a grill has a small amount of carcinogen called Creosote enzymes in rosemary and red wine do wonders to break down this

Directions:

In a mixing bowl add your ground meat and blend the two together by hand. Add your egg, rosemary, Worcestershire, onion, salt, pepper and garlic and continue to mix by hand. Then add your bread crumbs, rosemary and continue to mix. Put your mixed burger meat in the fridge for 30 minutes to cool and set. After the meat has set you form patties they should be around half a pound. The burgers should be about four inches in diameter and a hole should be pressed into the middle of the patty which allows for quicker cooking and the ability to check the doneness of the burger.

On a hot grill you want to sear the burgers just like a steak. A layer of caramelization will lock in the juices and your burger will be infinitely more moist. I like cooking my burger to medium because I am a human being and eating a burn to a crisp puck of beef is wrong on so many levels. But because the Canadian Beef Industry likes to add delicious bacteria to their meat, cooking to well is the only thing I recommend on this blog.

In a pan add your pea meal bacon with some olive oil. Pea meal bacon is a back cut of bacon crusted with well…pea meal. Everyone likes bacon on a burger but regular bacon has been overdone. Back bacon is great and on a burger it adds a ton of flavour. Retain the bacon fat and fry the eggs in the fat/oil mix. I like them over easy because Sunny Side is so delicate.

Building the burger: This is a delicate mission that uses many architectural principles. Here is the order of how things should be stacked. Bottom bun, Vietnamese Vaseline, Arugula, pickle, mustard, burger, cheese, pea meal bacon, tomato, egg, more Vietnamese Vaseline, top bun. And there you have it. The Braised Blue Burger!

Recipe Redux

Burgers are a truly North American dish. But sometimes you need a european take on a more renown american varietal. Primativo is the old world name for Zinfandel. This grape was originally cultivated in Croatia and is genetically one of the most ancient varietals still in wide use around the world. In Italy Primativo is grown in a few distinct regions but for this dish I would recommend one from Apulia at the South Eastern part of Italy*. Unlike a California Zinfandel, Italian Primativo is very dry and peppery. It works well with beef and pork. Zinfandel is normally looked at as a great utilitarian BBQ wine and it's Italian cousin adds a more aggressive yet refined take on the varital.

Foods You Should Know: Bison

Before the 20th century the American Bison was a huge source of meat in North America. These large nomadic grazing mammals are closely related to cattle. By the end of the 19th century American Bison were on the brink of extinction because of over hunting.

After about a hundred years of protection and breeding American Bison has made a comeback. While at the same time their meat made a return to north american kitchens as a environmental, culinary and health conscience beef alternative.

The American Bison also known as The American Buffalo*, for thousands of years roamed and grazed on the North American plains. From as far North as Great Slave Lake in the Northwest Territories in Canada to as far South as the Mexican regions of Durango and Nuevo Leon, as far West as the Sierra Madre, and as far East as Kentucky and Tennessee. This huge area of inhabitation made these animals very well suited to handle all kinds of different environments.**

Over the past few decades farmers have began to raise Bison for their meat. In this time they found that Bison took less work to produce more meat. Since Bison have evolved to eat many different types of plant matter they can be allowed to graze over large and less developed swaths of land. The Bison also are usually raised without the aid of hormones, antibiotics and other chemicals because they can feed on more wild grasses and they have evolved to be resistant to local disease***. As well because of the Bison's more wide ranged diet they don't need to travel as far for food, this means that there is less work that goes into herding them. Which makes their production have a smaller carbon footprint than cattle.

Bison Meat is also quite healthy as compared to beef for a number of reasons. First is that it contains about 1/3rd of the fat of beef. One serving of Bison has nearly all of your daily intake of Iron, and Zinc. It also offers the minimum daily intake of Selenium which is a mineral we rarely get enough of and affects the production of brain chemicals effecting anxiety and depression. When you take this all into account along with the hormone free, antibiotic free, and organic production methods that are commonly used in Bison farming it really is a great product to use in your kitchen.

There are a few draw backs to adding Bison to your diet. First is the expense. It is commonly between 20% and 75% more expensive than beef depending on where you live in Canada or the United States. This pricing difference is most due to the economics of how we get our food.

In Canada cattle farmers have been subsidized by the government to produce beef for decades, and because of this the production and distribution of beef has become streamlined and cheap. We produce too much, and because of that, the quality of the meat suffers. I am not saying Canada produces bad beef, I am saying that mass production and distribution of any fresh food product leads to its homogenization and movement towards a lower quality product. Bison has yet to really be factory farmed and we can see in its quality that unless you are getting premium or gourmet Canadian beef products there is a marked difference between ground bison and packaged ground beef.

As the above paragraph will illustrate, bison meat can be quite dry, if not prepared properly. Because of its low fat content bison needs to be cooked a little bit differently.

Bison Preparation Tip #1.

When browning ground bison I recommend pinching off slightly larger chunks of the ground meat. These bigger pieces have less surface area and will cook slower than finely minced meat. As well I find that browning bison at a lower heat than you would beef really helps to preserve the fat in the meat. Even starting your pan with a tiny bit of grape seed oil can make all the difference as the blend of the oil and the fat will raise the smoke point and you will get a lot less fat burning in the pan.

Bison Preparation Tip #2.

When dealing with a Bison steak. It is important to get a really nice sear on the meat. This will go a long way in locking in the juices. I like to heat up one side of the barbecue on high and the other on low to medium. Sear the steaks on one side of the grill and then transfer them to the cooler side of the grill and cooking them to medium rare or rare. Sorry people who like things well done, bison needs to be a bit under or you will lose the tiny but important bit of fat in the steak.

Bison Preparation Tip #3.

I believe I've done a piece on making stock****. So I will skip the how-to   but using bison bones to make stock is a great idea. If you are lucky enough to have a butcher who can sell you some bison marrow bones you can make a super rich and interesting stock. Just roast the bones and then add them to a pot of water and other ingredients and you can have a wonderful way to infuse that bison flavour into your dishes.

So I think this is about enough of our friend, the bison.

*A misnomer of sorts, as Buffalo is commonly used to describe The American Bison's African cousin the Water Buffalo.

**Sadly they were poorly suited to escaping white men with rifles.

***Domesticated Cattle have their origins in Turkey and the Middle East. They have evolved with a diet that is totally foreign to North America. Over the past 500 or so years, the ecological make up of North American has been changed by the addition of invasive plant species. Some of these invasive species were brought from Europe for the purpose of the production of beef. The ecosystem of the North American grass lands has totally transformed because of European settlement but the American Bison is still alive and kicking.

****I totally made this footnote up, I have yet to do a blog post on creating a simple stock and I am totally admitting it in my book. I will keep this in mind for Braised Blue: The Dark Meat Returns.

*Why do I make the distinction of using Danish Blue Cheese? It's a more mild blue cheese unlike Stilton or Gorgonzola but still quite creamy. It also works very well with fruit.

**You can used fresh or dried figs just know that dried figs have more concentrated sugar so they will probably work better but it's not necessary.

A different take on the Braised Blue Burger just with the addition of Danish Blue Cheese* and a few other goodies to give a different spin on the burger this summer.

Ingredients:

Refer to the Braised Blue Burger on page 43 for the ingredients for the Braised Blue Burger patty.

1 cup Danish blue cheese (crumbled)

2 Figs (diced)**

1 Onion (diced)

Arugula

Directions:

In a mixing bowl add your ground meat and blend the two together by hand. Add your egg, 1/2 cup of Danish blue cheese, Worcestershire, onion, salt, pepper and garlic and continue to mix by hand. Then add your bread crumbs, rosemary and continue to mix. Put your mixed burger meat in the fridge for 30 minutes to cool and set. After the meat has set you form patties they should be around half a pound. The burgers should be about four inches in diameter and a hole should be pressed into the middle of the patty which allows for quicker cooking and the ability to check the doneness of the burger.

In an oiled pan on medium/low heat, add your onions and sweat them, add your diced figs and cook until the sugars of the figs and the onion begin to meld this should take about 10 minutes.

Now once you have your patty formed you put your burgers on the grill and cook them like normal burgers, the blue cheese will begin to melt and hopefully if the grill is hot enough the cheese will begin to get crusty. When the burgers are almost finished crumble some more blue cheese onto the top, then take your onion and fig mixture and top the blue cheese. Once the cheese is melted take the burgers off the grill. And build your burger, I like to put some arugula, and dijon mustard to go with the burger.

Foods You Should Know: Civeche

Consuming raw seafood can be a daunting task for the beginner foodie but a Latin American dish can be a great gateway to new food experience and not to mention just an amazingly fresh and clean flavoured way to prepare your favourite seafood.

This Central and South American technique of using citrus juice to cook seafood is a great way of putting a twist on fresh seafood. The word Civeche comes from the Spanish word Escabeche which means "to Pickle", though the technique of using the acidity of citrus fruit to cook meat is not a European technique, It comes from the indigenous peoples of coastal Central and South America.

Making Civeche is actually a pretty simple preparation but what you for sure need is fresh seafood i.e. white low oil fish like mackerel or tilapia, squid, octopus, scallop, or shrimp. Lime or Lemon Juice is then added to the seafood and tossed this will begin the cooking process, salt for seasoning, then other regional/seasonal ingredients are added to the marinade. Of course, as I have said many times, simple does not mean easy. Civeche is all about timing and making the dish to order, but there is literally nothing like a perfectly made Civeche.

Like most other foods I've talked about in this blog, Civeche is a very regional dish. Depending on where the style originates from and what is seasonally fresh you can have a huge variation in what goes into a typical Civeche.

In Peru, who's national dish is Civeche, there are literally hundreds of different regional/seasonal Civeches that range from light and almost perfumed to exceptionally creamy and in some cases incredibly spicy. Sea Bass, octopus and squid are common.

In Mexico we see Civeche that includes avocado, chilies, salsa, and tortilla chips to use as a scoop in many cases.

In Ecuador where they have an exceptionally acidic type of tomato use the juice of this tomato in place of citrus to create a red Civeche. As well they use oysters, and barnacles to create a super earthy flavoured dish.

Panamanian Civeche is much like Mexican Civeche but they serve it with a puff pastry called Canastitas.

Cuban Civeche normally will include Mahi Mahi or Tuna.

Now Civeche isn't always the best choice. Freshness is paramount and eating bad fish or shellfish can be a very dangerous proposition. This is why trusting your local fishmonger or restaurant is key before you eat a raw application of seafood. Even though the flesh has been slightly cooked by the citrus there can still be many types of bacteria, and parasites present. So it really isn't a totally safe application. But if you want to leave on the wild side and push your food boundaries than civeche is a great dish to try.

If you haven't noticed you are in the Burger section of this cookbook. This recipe is a little but more akin to burger cos-play*. When people think of California they think of fresh ingredients, seafood and a Mexican influence. This burger is a really easy way to take pretty much the same burger as I did last week but make it a little bit healthier and just as delicious. Pretty much, you're using the same patty as the Original burger but you will be dressing it down and rebuilding it. You will be making a Guacamole and then a cheese and shrimp stuffed fresno chili to top the burger with. Both of these applications are simple and really delicious.

The Guacamole:

Ingredients:

3-Avocados (halved, skinned, pitted)

1 Lime (juiced)

Sea salt

1/2 tbs Cumin

2 Serrano chilies (seeded, cored, diced)

1/2 Onion (diced)

2 Roma tomatoes (diced)

1 clove Garlic (diced)

Cilantro

Directions: In a mixing bowl crush the avocado with lime juice and salt. The acid in the lime will stop the avocado from oxidizing and turning brown**. You want to leave the avocado a little bit chunky. You then add your cumin, peppers, onion, tomato, garlic and cilantro. Mix gently, making sure that the guacamole is nice and thick and chunky. Cover and refrigerate.

*Whenever I hear the term Cos Play all I can imagine is people in Cosby sweaters and dwarfs dressed up as Rudy. Yah, I just made things weird didn't I?

**Brown avocado does not make a difference flavour wise but it doesn't look very good and lime works well with the flavour profile.

The Stuffed Fresno Chilis:

Ingredients:

4 Fresno chilies (slit down one side, cored and seeded)

1.5 cups Monterey jack cheese (grated)

1 cup Shrimp (diced)

2 Limes (juiced)

Sea salt

Black pepper

Directions: In a bowl take your diced shrimp and toss them with the lime juice. You are essentially creating a ceviche*** with the shrimp. You take your peppers out to the grill and blister them until their skin can be easily removed. Carefully remove the skin of the pepper and lay them out flat on a cutting board. You then fill the pepper with the ceviche and grated Monterey Jack, some sea salt, and ground black pepper. In parchment paper wrap the filled peppers. On the top rack of your barbecue while you're grilling your burgers put the paper wrapped peppers and allow them to heat up and the cheese to melt.

Building the Burger: Here is how this burger goes together. Bun-Guacamole-Patty-Stuffed pepper-Guacamole-Bun. If it seems simple it's because it is simple. Enjoy.

Recipe Redux

This burger is a Mexi-Cali take on the above Braised Blue Burger and pairing a wine with it shows how different I like to go with my pairings. The addition of avocado, and ceviche to this burger makes for tougher pairing. I love to add some texture and some intense aromatics to the dish with the wine. For this I would chose a wine from Spain. A Ribera del Deuro to be more specific. This wine hailing from the northern Spanish plateau land along the Deuro river is a great match for this dish. With an aggressive nose of earth and cigar box, Ribera Del Deuro also boasts a very intense tannic mouth feel that can at times be puckering, but this mouth feel will really work with with the creaminess of the avocado and the acidity of the ceviche stuffed pepper.

Recipe: Tijuana Shrimp Tacos w/ Peanut and Avocado Salsa

When people think Tacos they thing greasy ground beef, marinaded steak using the name Carne Asada, or flavourless Refried beans. There is a whole country of different Mexican flavours that are unexpected and delicious. Today I am going to show you how to make an authentic Tijuana Style Shrimp Taco with a peanut guacamole salsa*. It's super simple to make and really delicious.

The Tacos

Ingredients:

10 Tiger shrimp (cut width wise in inch long pieces)

1 Lime (juiced)

Olive oil

Vegetable stock

Onions (diced)

1 Cloves garlic (crushed with salt)

1 Tomato (diced/strained)

5 Arbol chilis

1 tbs Mexican oregano

Directions: In an oiled pan on medium heat put your dry arbol chilies and roast them until they become soft and remove them from the pan. This will leave really nice roasted pepper flavour in the oil and it will flavour the rest of the dish without it being too aggressively spicy. Then put in your onions and sweat them. Add you oregano, lime juice, and garlic. Let those integrate then add your tomato. Deseed, core and dice your arbol chilies very finely and add them back to the pan. When the contents of the pan begin to caramelize add half a cup of stock to deglaze and increase your heat to medium/high reduce again for about 5 minutes. Then add your shrimp tjand sauté for about 4 minutes. The heat in the pan should easily cook the small hunks of shrimp without much trouble.

* This sounds like a weird mix but the texture play that is going but also a great acidity that will life this dish into a different atmosphere.

The Salsa:

Ingredients:

1 Avocado

2 Tbs Peanuts

Cilantro

2 Serrano chilies

2 tbs lime juice

Directions: In a blender add all of your ingredients and blend to a puree. Yup, it's that easy. Press a button, salsa is made. The combo of Peanut and avocado is really amazing. Rich, smooth, and delightfully fresh.

Bringing it Together: On a griddle place your corn* tortillas, double them up and place some cheese between them. Get some nice colour on the tortilla then place more cheese on top, then your shrimp, then a nice dollop of the salsa. Remove from the griddle, fold and eat. Remember that tacos should be a huge mess and if they aren't a huge mess you are doing it wrong.

*Corn is always better

Recipe Redux
This dish is a little tough to pair. You have a lot of balance on the plate so the wine should pair a little more with the flavour profile and textures of the dish than to fill a hole. I would go with an Beringer Founder's Estate Chardonnay. It's a Napa Chardonnay that sees medium oaking but also retains a really nice amount of acidity and brightness. It's green apple and tropical fruit interplay will work well with this dish.

Foods You Should Know: Regional American BBQ...A Porktorial Thesis

Before I even start this piece I need to make this very clear. Grilling and Barbecue are two different things. When you make a steak you are grilling, when you make a brisket you are barbecuing. What is the main difference? In a word…smoke. Your home barbecue is probably only used as a grill especially if it runs on gas, you cook your burgers, steaks and chicken. Now if you took that same barbecue, added some wood chips or charcoal, never let the heat get above 250 and smoked a pork shoulder for six hours, you are barbecuing.

The word Barbecue comes from the native South American word barbacot which translates to "wooden rack", which refers to the technique of these native people of placing their meat on a wooden rack above a fire. Spanish explorers (genociders*) brought the technique to North America and it was quickly taken on by the colonists.

Now, barbecue comes from all over the world. Korea, Australia, the UK, Canada, France, the Caribbean, and South Africa to name a few. Today we are going to talk about my favourite theocracy to the south, The United States of America.** American Barbecue is ultra regional and cannot really be defined as one thing. Along the Mississippi, barbecue works like the blues, similar DNA but every city has their own take on it***. Kansas City represents the midwestern sensibility. The Carolinas are still fighting a civil war over barbecue, and Texas is well...Texas.

So what makes regional American BBQ so different? If I was to stumble my way into a Pan-American BBQ cook off how can I not look like a dumbshit?****

Kansas City BBQ:

We will start with my least favourite of the four main styles. Kansas City BBQ is all about the sauce, KC Masterpiece anyone? Kansas City BBQ sauce is a heavy mixture of molasses and tomato sauce, it is not my cup of tea, but there are some good aspects of Kansas City BBQ. Kansas City is an equal opportunity meat eating town. Pork, beef, chicken, turkey and fish all get included which is cool. What isn't cool is on your nice smoked chicken leg gets covered in their BBQ spackle. The most prized thing in Kansas City BBQ is the burnt ends of the meat, because of the thick sauce and heavy smoked used in the process the bark on the outside of the meat can be glorious. Overall Kansas City BBQ isn't my favourite but it may be the most widely known style of American BBQ.

Memphis BBQ:

In the early days of The Blues, musicians would travel up and down the the Mississippi River from Chicago to New Orleans. This migration would allow musicians to hear the regional music and tailor the blues to each region. Over time this practice of using local folk music as a flavour for the structure of The Blues stratified the music scene along the Mississippi, Chicago Blues sounds almost nothing like Delta Blues.

BBQ along the Mississippi is the same way. Cooking techniques, ingredients and flavours all colour the BBQ along the Mississippi. Memphis BBQ seems to have come up as the winner. Memphis is the most democratic of the BBQ styles. It offers a wet and a dry style of BBQ. The Dry is comprised of a dry rubbed piece of meat being smoked for hours on a pit BBQ and sauce is kept within 500 yards of the dry style. The wet style BBQ is basted with a tomato and vinegar based sauce which is less sweet than Kansas City style. Usually the wet ribs are then dipped into more sauce while being eaten. Memphis is all about inclusion, wet or dry you can have your choice.

Carolina BBQ:

Carolina BBQ is like the Middle East, with fewer teeth and more pork. There is a bunch of people who fundamentally disagree with each other on how to make BBQ and I assume that there are styles of Carolina that have been lost to history because their proponents were wiped off the earth. So here is my attempt at breaking this all down.

North Carolina:

Eastern vs Lexington: Eastern Carolina BBQ is all about full animal BBQ. This means that the entire pig is cooked on a spit and then chopped up(along with the skin) into a delicious porky slurry of meat and cracklin'. While Lexington style is all about the pork shoulder. They smoke the shoulder for as long as 24 hours and then shred it. It is the ultimate pulled pork. Lexington BBQ

South Carolina:

Like Eastern Carolina, all of the South Carolina BBQ is based on whole hog cooking. Central Carolina uses a mustard based sauce which was derived from German immigrants who settled in the area. Western South Carolina uses a tomato and hot pepper based sauce. Finally Piedmonte uses a vinegar and pepper based sauce which works more as a mop to create a great bark on the meat.

Texas BBQ:

Finally Texas BBQ is a different animal. It is mostly beef based though against popular belief pork is still acceptable. There are four main styles of Texas BBQ. East Texas eats more like Kansas City style. In Central Texas style BBQ we again see German influence, the meat is usually of a higher quality and a thin vinegar based sauce is used. In West Texas we see more of a frontier style BBQ. It's all about smoke and heat over mesquite wood, this area is almost 100% beef and normally dry rubs are employed. In Southern Texas we see the Mexican influence creep into the cuisine. Dry rubs, peppers, mole, etc all become part of the BBQ culture.

In all, BBQ is an art and like any art it's the environment which helps shape the final product.

---

*Sorry for the downer but can you really be a downer when you're talking BBQ?

**That was kind of mean eh? If Barbecue was the dominant religion in the US, I think it would be a better place, care to disagree?

***Though Memphis usually gets the credit for perfecting the Mississippi style of BBQ. St. Louis does great things, as does New Orleans. And I would like to add in a few cities on the Ohio River as well, Cincinnati and Lexington have some great BBQ as does Louisville.

****Well you are currently reading this which puts you ahead of many of those who would be frequenting a Pan-American BBQ Cook-off. But knowing your Piedimonte from your Lexington will probably get you all kind of street cred.

Pork Tenderloin is a great cut to work with, it's inexpensive, versatile, flavourful, and pretty forgiving. I like to think of it as a blank canvas of pork that you can infused pretty much any flavour into.

Ingredients: 1 Pork tenderloin (trimmed of silver-skin on the outside of the cut)

Salt

Black pepper

2 oz Bourbon

Tomato paste

1 clove Garlic (chopped and crushed)

Juice of one lemon

2 tbs Brown sugar

Olive oil

Crushed red pepper

Chili powder

1 Large ziplock bag

Directions: In a mixing bowl add bourbon, lemon juice, and garlic and allow the garlic to macerate for five to ten minutes into the liquid. Add Red Pepper flakes, and olive oil, brown sugar, and chili powder. The mixture will still be quite watery. You then add Tomato paste until the mixture becomes more of a paste. Add Salt and pepper to taste. Then put your tenderloin into the Ziplock bag and your BBQ marinade as well. Leave in the fridge marinating for 2 hours. Remove the tenderloin and let sit at room temperature for 30 minutes before grilling. By this time the meat should have pulled a lot of the moisture out of the marinade and the remaining liquid can be used to baste the tenderloin as it cooks. Place the tenderloin on a very hot grill and sear it on all sides. Bring the head down and let the tenderloin cook until it reaches medium. Turning and basting in sauce every so often. This should take about 30-40 minutes depending on the thickness of the cut and the heat of the grill. Cut into the middle of the tenderloin to check for pinkness if necessary, because of the denseness of the meat you won't lose a ton of moisture. When finished let the Tenderloin rest for ten minutes and then cut to serve with your baked beans.

In the end the tenderloin should have a crust on the outside of smokey, sweet, and tangy flavour profile, which is the perfect compliment to the richness of the BBQed baked beans. Give it a try this summer.

Normally when I write a recipe I do an entire meal. I am much too hung over and sleep deprived to do that*. So I am going to give you the low down on a simple and fast side dish that will blow your mind.

Ingredients:

1 can Black beans (strained and rinsed in cold water)

5 slices Bacon (cut into half inch wide pieces)

3 tps Grainy mustard

1 cup Ketchup

2 oz Bourbon

1 tbs Balsamic vinegar

1 tsp Sriracha sauce (or any hot sauce of your choice)

Directions:

In a pot render your sliced bacon at medium high heat. I like to make it pretty crispy as it will be sitting in a bunch of sauce and a little crunch from the bacon adds some nice texture. Then add your beans. Let the beans and bacon really marry together. Don't worry if the beans are mushy they will taste like bacon and that is a good thing.** Add the bourbon to deglaze the bacon and beans. As the bourbon evaporates add the vinegar, ketchup, hot sauce and mustard. Let the mixture simmer for about thirty minutes and let those flavours really develop. You will end up with a smokey, bacon-y but nicely acidic bean dish. The mustard and vinegar balance the richness and the sweetness of the other ingredients. And the mustard grains almost pop like caviar as you eat.

* I will release another post about my Toronto weekend but there is some pretty good wear and tear on my brain from a few too many scotches and beers last night. I figured a recipe would be something low key but rewarding.

**Fuck, did I just write that? I wonder if there is a Martha Stewart: Hangovers.

In Vino Veritas: Judging The Juice By The Label

The business of branding wine is actually operates like pretty much any other business, just in an exaggerated way. Because there is so much competition and because it is a high volume product wine lives and dies by its ability to catch the consumer's eye. The brands that are successful are so rarely the best products that many true wine lovers have to divorce themselves from being consumers in such an exaggerated way that they become known as snobs.*

What makes a wine successful?

Price: I cannot stress this point enough, price rules liquor sales. The vast majority of customers want whatever is cheap or on sale that week. Cheap wine is 99 times out of 100 a low quality wine, just like cheap beer or cheap vodka. The only cheap wine that is high quality is unprofitable wine.

History: Gallo has been around for as long as American wine has been relevant. Everyone knows the brand and most people equate familiarity to quality. The problem is that Gallo and their other brands do not make high quality wines. What they really mean is they have been the lowest common denominator for years.**

Labeling: Wines with memorable names and labels sell better than great wines trying to sell on their own merits. It's everything that our mom's told us not to do growing up. Judging a book by its cover. Countless times, in retail, I was faced with a group of half drunk twenty something women who want to drink Girls Night Out, or Little Black Dress. These are both horrendous wines, but they have succeeded in capturing an important piece of the market by having cute labels with very specifically targeted names.

1. Pitch the Bitch: If you market to women your wine will be more successful. Women generally drink more wine than men, they also statistically spend less on wine than men. But here is the catch, men buy wine that they think women will like because, men like to have sex with women who are drunk on wine. No guy wants to drink or buy a wine with a cartoon penguin on the label, but they do. No guy wants to drink or buy a wine called Seduction, who's bottle looks like a corset, but they do. Women are the target of wine sales because both women and men buy wine marketed towards women.***

2. Animals and Other Cutesy Shit: Countless numbers of times you will encounter wine customers who have no idea what kind of wine they want to buy, other than the fact that they vaguely remember a kangaroo on the label. This is how Yellowtail gets away with taking a dump in bottles and calling it wine. If you can handle your product being called, "That cat piss wine," or "The foot wine," or even "the one with the cactus on the bottle," than you will be successful. If your wine's name isn't memorable, sometimes you just need to use something that has nothing to do with wine or even something that should not have anything to do with wine to make your product memorable.

3. Dress It Up: This is a marketing tactic as old as time. Putting lipstick on a pig. If you have a low quality wine and you want it to beat the wines in its pricing category as well as take market share from premium wine. All you need to do is make your low quality wine look like a premium. A heavier or slightly taller bottle, labels that are striking, and names that sound majestic are all ways to premiumize a non premium product. Vincor's Copper Moon does this amazingly well. It's a slightly heavier grade of glass, the label is modern and clean so it stands out on the shelf from most of the other Canadian wine, and the name stays with you. It's gut rotting swill that I wouldn't subject a sewer to, but it succeeds because it looks more expensive than its similarly priced competition.

The reason I am telling you all of this is because I want people to drink good wine. The more people learn about how something is sold to them, the more likely people will support smaller wine operations who focus on making great products. I strive to support winemakers who care about their craft, not the marketing. But, when it comes to making money to support your craft, understanding how wine is sold is a great tool to have in your belt.

*There are wine snobs and then there are wine assholes. I am comfortable being a wine snob and offering small tidbits to the less educated as to allow them to make a more informed decision. Wine assholes like to show off their expensive collections but know nothing about wine. This would be akin to a person who owns a Porsche Panamera with an automatic transmission telling somebody who has lovingly restored a classic Alpha Romeo that he should totally get something newer.

**I kind of hate to pick on Gallo because they run a tight business (and they are not the only ones who do this), but they are exactly what I am talking about when it comes to great branding trumping quality. Without apology, Gallo makes sub-premium products, and many of those you may drink and not even know it. Barefoot, Apothic, Dancing Bull, Carlo Rossi, and McWilliams are all Gallo brands, and no real wine person would go within a mile of them.

*** We see this flipped on its head when it comes to beer. Beer is mostly marketed to men, but women also buy beer marketed to men because they want to make their boyfriend/husband happy. And presumably to get laid, but I assume that it is much less of a determining factor.

Foods You Should Know: Salmon

Salmon is one of my favourite kinds of fish to eat. It's a dense, oily, rich species of fish but not all kinds of Salmon are equal. Today's Foods You Should Know will talk about all things Salmon.

Types of Salmon:

The term Salmon derives from the latin, Salmo which means to jump, there are nine species of fish commonly recognized as Salmon. Seven of them are closely related and two are kind of odd balls that get the name Salmon but really don't share much with the seven core species.

The Seven Core Species:

Chinook Salmon

Chum Salmon

Coho Salmon

Pink Salmon

Sockeye Salmon

Steelhead Trout

Masu Salmon

The Two Associated Species.

Atlantic Salmon

Danube Salmon

The seven core species have much darker coloured meat, with denser oilier characteristics. They are generally considered better flavoured fish, that taste better, with much more nutritional value. Steelhead Trout is kind of a strange addition as most people don't see it as a Salmon. But the species is actually genetically much closer to tout than their exclusively fresh water dwelling namesakes. The Atlantic Salmon is a commonly used salmon because they are easy to farm raise but their quality is much lower than the more proper salmon, but we will get more into that in the next section.

Farm Raised vs Wild

Many people don't know what exactly they are eating when they eat fish. Much of what you buy from your super market isn't just questionable when it comes to freshness. It's also questionable when it comes to the methods of their production. Factory farming doesn't just apply to livestock.   The Atlantic Salmon you get in the supermarket is farm raised. The flesh of the fish is a light pink* and the density of the meat is much less. Farm raised fish are also more likely to suffer from disease because they are penned much to close to each other so large amounts of antibiotics must be used to keep them healthy and growing.   It has been observed that the amount of dioxin and PCBs in farmed salmon is at times 8 times higher than wild salmon. There actually has been a movement in farming Coho Salmon which has actually bore great results compared to Atlantic Salmon or Steelhead Trout.

Wild Salmon is usually smaller, the meat is bright reddish pink**, the meat is much denser and flavourful. They are much less likely to suffer from disease and they are free from antibiotics. Salmon are also a relatively fast growing fish that can get quite large. Slower growing fish, like tuna, accumulate heavy metals and chemicals in their systems over time. Wild Salmon are much better when it comes to their safety. The health benefits of Wild Salmon greatly out weighs that of farmed fish. Wild Salmon is also a much more sustainable resource than farmed salmon as long as quotas and ethical practices are used in their fishing.

Health Benefits:

Salmon are one of the healthiest species of fish. They are high in Omega 3 fatty acids and are a great source of EPA and DHA which are the toughest at the Omega 3 fatty acids to find in the diet. They are also one of the only foods that are a source of vitamin D3. These brain nourishing compounds help prevent depression and anxiety, as well the synthesis of neurotransmitters and other chemicals and proteins in the brain. Salmon is true brain food.

Salmon is also high in Low Density Lipoprotein also known as "good cholesterol." Which also makes it's heart healthy. The best part of it all is that it is delicious.

*Wild Salmon get their bright colour from a diet of krill. Farm raised salmon have a feed diet so they lose the bright hue in their flesh.

**Salmon coloured even.

Recipe: Philly Cedar Plank Smoked Salmon w/ Marinated Shiitake Mushrooms and Micro-green Salad

*If this was Emeril Lagasse's cook book this footnote would have included a Leopold "Boom" reference.

**Bread Crumbs are the secret to this dish. They bind your filling together, otherwise the heat would cause the cheese to melt and run all over your cedar plank. They also get a nice crust on the filling after some of that salmon oil begins to ooze out of the fish.

So the title of this piece is the Ulysses of food blog titles*, but if you have the time and fortitude to get through this title you will be rewarded by this dish. It's one of my favorites and it's much simpler than the title.

The Salmon: What you will need is Salmon Steaks, I will not go into the importance of buying wild salmon in another blog post but suffice it to say, Wild Salmon, tastes better, it cooks better and it's much better for you.

Salmon steaks

Salt

Pepper

Cream cheese

Fresh rosemary

1 Lemon

Bread crumbs

One soaked cedar plank (I soak for 24 hours, because I find high heat works better for cedar smoking.)

How to: Take the cream cheese and stir in the fresh rosemary and bread crumbs**. As you are mixing zest the lemon into the mixture. Take the cream cheese filling and stuff the Salmon Steak better the two dorsal horns of the cut. Then take butcher's twine and tie the entire cut together circumference wise. You want the cream cheese filling to be packed in very tight. This also keeps the salmon steak compressed which will help this normally thick cut cook much more evenly. You then put the fish on your cedar plank which should be still damp, and to the grill you go. Normally salmon steaks take about 45 minutes to cook on the plank, but it's really about letting the technique take it's time and really set that smokey flavour and caramelization of the outside of the meat. If the fish seems to be drying out placing some slices of that lemon I mentioned earlier can help. I personally like to grill some sliced lemon as a garnish.

The Salad:

Ingredients:

Shitake mushrooms

Sherry vinegar

Soy sauce

Salt

Whole black peppercorns

Dill

Micro arugula

Directions:

Submerge the mushrooms in boiling water for about 15 minutes. Strain the mushrooms over a container and keep the reserve liquid for later. Then take the mushrooms in a sauce pan adding the salt, pepper corns, and dill to the sherry vinegar and soy sauce. Reduce the mixture and de-glaze your pan with the reserve liquid which you saved from earlier. Simmer and reduce by half. Then take the mixture and refrigerate. Serve the mushrooms on a bed of micro arugula.

This entire dish is my play on two sushi dishes. The Philadelphia Roll and The Shitake Roll. As a whole the fish component of the dish is quite rich. I like pairing it with the salad because there is great acidity which kind of cuts the richness. On the plate the dish looks pretty austere, the stuffed fish and the small salad can be pretty stark and minimalist once again bringing back the aesthetic of sushi.

Recipe Redux: There is a long standing belief that fish and red wine do not mix. This could not be further from the truth when it comes to oily fish and smoked fish. Think of this as the Captain Kirk kissing Nyota Uhura, moment in your culinary life.* I would suggest 2010 Argyle Pinot Noir from the Willamette Valley in Oregon. It's a light bodied new world style take on pinot noir. Lots of strawberry and wild mushroom notes, with a nice acid balance. The flavours do well into interplay with the oily smokey fish and the tart salad.

*If you didn't get this reference I don't blame you because it is a Star Trek reference and I even think it was poorly advised. But here it goes, the first interracial kiss on television was between William Shatner and Nichelle Nichols on Star Trek. I still feel dirty, but my white guilt is lifting away.

Foods You Should Know: Sushi

Since I've moved back to Ontario I've noticed that Sushi doesn't hold the same place in the general population's heart as it did in Calgary.* To be frank, I don't even know where the best sushi places in the Windsor area are**, I know what UrbanSpoon tells me.*** But I am also not going to go into every hole in the wall sushi place to brave lukewarm sashimi and haphazardly dolled out wasabi paste. Please refer to the glossary at the bottom of the article so that you can keep up.

Sushi Fears

Japanese Cuisine is an adventure. It dares you to take your preconceived notions about food and then turns them on their heads.

1. It's cold food. In North American there is an aversion to a cold plate of food, unless it's a salad. Japanese cuisine isn't all cold and I've had cooked sushi rolls which were stunning, but it's something you mentally have to get past. Try simple things first, or something familiar, once you get it…you'll get it.

2. There is raw fish, am I going to get sick? Probably not, sushi restaurants will not survive long if they serve substandard products. Yes it's raw, but a trained sushi chef can tell if a cut of fish is not safe to eat and anyone worth a damn with never serve bad meat, much less raw bad meat.

3. I don't know what anything on the menu means. That is the point. It's a menu not a readers digest, put it away. Treat your visit like an adventure, ask your server questions or for some recommendations, try new things, and order a bunch of stuff. If you don't like something ,usually it comes in a small enough portion that you're not going to starve.

Braised Blue Recommends

I truly believe that jumping in feet first is the best way to get into anything that you are unsure of. Sushi is totally like this. Here are my tips:

1. Get yourself a bowl of miso soup: because it's something that will introduce you to some of the flavours you can expect with the rest of the meal, but in a very approachable way. Miso soup is comfort food, it's warm and inviting, the aromas put you at ease.

2. If you order California Rolls hang your head in shame: This is like going to a steakhouse and ordering a Chicken Caesar. Sure it's on the menu, and you know you like it, this does not mean you need to order it. Save a California Roll order for lunch time at the grocery store, some pimple faced white kid, in a smock, can make you one.

3. Communicate with your server: Sure it's at times easier said than done, but if you ask your server what the chef recommends it shows that you care. The chef knows what is fresh, the chef knows what he does well. Trust these people to steer you in the right direction.

4. Just Eat It: I would never had known I loved sea urchin until I grabbed a random piece of sushi off of a plate at a work party. I ate the rest of them. Knowing what you are eating can psych you out, sometimes just allowing yourself to experiment will help you figure out what you like.

5. Show your appreciation: Tipping your server and sushi chef is customary and it may get you some free sushi the next time you come in. I always make it a point to greet and thank the chef and make it clear that I am tipping him.

Glossary:

Sushi: A Japanese food consisting of cooked vinegared rice topped or rolled with other ingredients. There are three main types of Sushi that you will see pretty much every where in North America, Nigirizushi, Makizushi, and Temaki.

Nigirizushi: A hand formed clump of rice usually topped with fish or veggies. Unagi(fresh water eel) is one of the most known types of Nirigizushi.

Makizushi: Rolled sushi. This is a common style that you will see everywhere. The famous and boring California Roll would be a great example of Makizushi

Temaki: Hand Roll. This of this as the tacone of the sushi world. Usually wrapped in nori, rice and all kind of other ingredients are rolled into kind of a cone shaped cigar of sushi.

Dashi: Japanese cooking stock, comprised of edible seaweed and dried fermented fish. The base of Miso soup, is also kind of a Japanese mother sauce and marinade.

Nori: Seaweed wrapper.

Sashimi: Not technically sushi. Sashimi is uncooked high grade finfish, shellfish, beef, etc, which are precisely cut to compliment the character of the meat. In most North American restaurants you will see. Salmon, Hamachi(japanese amberjack), Maguro(a genus of bluefin tuna, which has about a dozen different cuts)

Roe: Fish eggs, normally in North America you will find bright orange salmon roe used as a visual or textural aspect of a sushi roll.

In all, sushi is a healthy, flavorful and adventurous ethnic food. There is lots to learn about it and lots of taste. What I love about sushi is the unique and wild the textures, smells, flavours you get. I also love is how precise and beautiful the visual presentation of the food appears. Drop your defenses and preconceptions and give it a try.

---

*Or Vancouver, Seattle, San Francisco, etc.

** Sushi purists, veterans, snobs, this article is not for you. I am being general in this piece for the benefit of those who may not be familiar. So save your comments and judgements, unless you want me to shit down your throats in the comment section.

***I am not going to bash Urbanspoon, in a pinch it's a god send. I have found that the reviews aren't really helpful in anyway. I actually imagine the voices of the people complaining on Urbanspoon as shrill or somewhat mentally handicapped.

Recipe: Grilled Vegetable Towers w. Mustard Scallion Dressing.

*At what point do my readers notice the publishing date of this piece. I guess they will now.**

**Readers note, because I did not date the articles from my blog in this book I will let you in on this joke. I published this article on September 11th 2012. Now look at realize what you are making and recoil in horror or laugh your ass off. Your choice.

Today we have the second vegetarian dish in our Meatless Mondays inspired series. This one is more of a lunch dish unless you really want to make a second tower then maybe it would be enough for dinner*. This is meant to be a really rustic dish which kind of off plays warm and cold elements as well as jarringly powerful flavours of the tomato and dressing set against the subtle monolithic flavours of the grilled veggies.

The Tower

Ingredients:

1 Eggplant (sliced 1/2 inch thick)

1 Portobello mushroom

1 Tomato sliced thick.

Goat cheese

Provolone cheese

1 Cucumber (sliced very thin)

1 Zucchini (sliced thin)

Directions:

First and foremost your portobello mushroom is going to be the standard for width of the tower. It will be the base so when cutting your veggies keeping their diameter a little smaller than the diameter of the portobello is the best way to make sure your tower doesn't come down. Simple food engineering. Take your mushroom, eggplant and zucchini coat them in oil oil, add some salt and pepper and place them on the grill. You want to cook these well but not too far as they need to have some stability. The Zucchini should cook first, the eggplant a few minutes later and finally the portobello mushroom. So to start building your tower you lay the mushroom upside down(gill side up) fill the inside of the mushroom with goat cheese. Then layer the eggplant, then on top of the eggplant a slice of provolone. Then on top of the cheese you add a slice of tomato. Then more goat cheese on top of the tomato, then the grilled zucchini, then more provolone, then top with the thin sliced cucumber.

The Dressing

Ingredients:

Olive oil

Garlic

Scallions

1 tbs Grainy mustard

Balsamic vinegar

1 tsp mayonnaise.

Directions:

In a pan on medium/low heat. Add you oil and garlic. You then add your scallions and cook them down to the point of caramelization. You then pour off your infused oil into a container. Then add half the volume of the oil in balsamic vinegar, a tea spoon of mayo and a table spoon of grainy mustard. You then whisk the mixture until the oil and vinegar have emulsified by the mayo.

You then drizzle the dressing onto your tower, and enjoy.

Recipe Redux
Salad wines are always a bit of a tough go, but with this salad having warm grilled elements as well as the normal cold elements it opens up the playbook. William Knuttel Pinot Gris is a revelation for a white wine drinker. On its own it's a soft creamy almost nugetty expression of the Alsatian style of Pinot Gris. The same grape as the acidic and fresh Italian Pinot Grigio is left on the vines longer to mature and then sees a few months of oak to give the wine more presence and body. With the dish this wine actually balances against the acidity of the dressing and the smokey flavours of the grilled veggies perfectly. Enjoy.

There is an assumption that because most of my recipes are less than healthy that I don't cook healthy things. I really do have a pretty decent roster for healthy recipes. Today I am going to give you a recipe for a salad. This is not a side dish, this is a salad that happens to be a meal.

Ingredients:

1 Chicken breast

1 Handful of Pancetta

Mesclun greens

1 Avocado (sliced)

1/2 Cucumber (rounds)

2 Tomatoes (quartered)

Red onion (sliced)

Pecans

Brown sugar

Sea salt

Red chili flakes

Mustard powder

canola oil

Olive oil

Balsamic vinegar

Mayonnaise

Sriracha sauce (or like hot sauce)

Recipe Redux:

Wine and Salad is kind of a tricky pairing to make. Salads normally have more than enough acidity for one palate to take. So finding a wine that will work with the acidity and the textures in a salad can be a balancing act. With this salad, I would go with Mount Nelson Sauvignon Blanc from New Zealand. The wine is from famed wine maker Lodovico Antinori, he set out to make old world style Sauv Blanc from the high end fruit grown by the Kiwis. He succeeded in a big way. This wine can stand up to the meat, the sweetness of the pecan and the balsamic while giving you a grassy palette cleansing effect from the minerality and acidity of the wine.

Directions:

Part 1: The Chicken…

Rub chicken down with olive oil and rub with salt, pepper, mustard powered and red chili flakes. Place on a very hot Barbecue or Grill Pan. Sear all sides to create a crust and lock in juices. Cook until juices are clear. Let rest for five minutes and slice length wise into strips. It's not a bad thing to get a little bit of char on the chicken. It will work well with the flavours and textures of the salad.

Part 2: The Candied Pecans.

In a sauce pan melt butter with brown sugar, sea salt and red chili flakes. Once the sauce is uniform. Add the pecans. Make sure to coat the pecans in the sauce. Sauté the Pecans until the sauce begins to tighten. Remove from heat and pour the pecan/sauce mixture onto a cookie sheet. And place in a freezer for 15 minutes. Remove from Freezer and break up the pecan brittle.

Part 3: The balsamic emulsion*

In a bowl add 1/3 cup olive oil, 1/3 cup balsamic, 1 tsp of Mayonnaise, 1 splash of Sriracha Pepper Sauce.. Whisk for about 30 seconds or until the emulsion is uniform.

Part 4: Assembly.

In a large bowl add your lettuce, tomatoes, cucumber, and avocado. Then drizzle your balsamic emulsion over the salad. Then add your chicken slices, and pecan brittle. Drizzle a little more balsamic emulsion over the finished salad and you're ready for a very filling meal.

*Many people who make their own salad dressing run into the oil and vinegar separating and getting an uneven coating on their salad. Adding a little bit of Mayonnaise will act as a binding agent and cause the oil and vinegar to stay together for a longer period of time. This is called an emulsion. This will usually work for about 2 hours until the oil and vinegar separate. Shaking or whisking the mixture again will cause the emulsion to reform.(Hence shake before using.)

Recipe: Marinated Flank Steak, Garlic Sautéed Crimini Mushrooms and Double Green Puree.

Today, I wanted to come up with a great summer dish that was still substantial and also pretty easy. Though I think I may have failed at that, this should still be really good for your next dinner on the back patio.

The Steak

Ingredients:

1 Flank steak (1 kg or so)

2 cloves Garlic (finely chopped)

1/3 cup of Olive oil

100 ml Bourbon

2 tbs Balsamic vinegar

2 Leaves Sage

Black pepper (freshly ground)

Kosher salt

Recipe Redux

Flank steak screams for a big bold wine, it's a strong flavoured cut of beef and this recipe really brings out those big flavours. Your wine needs to stand up and deliver. My suggestion would be a Zinfandel from Sonoma County, California. More specifically I would recommend something from either Dry Creek Valley, or Alexander Valley. These wines pack a punch, lots of big fruit flavour, lots of alcohol and lots of spice make up the backbone of Sonoma Zinfandel. There are other areas of California that produce great Zin but when it comes to pairing with grilled meat Sonoma Zin is my choice and it should be yours.

Directions:

The night before get your Flank steak and score it on both sides with 1/4 of an inch cuts. In a bowl mix together the garlic, oil, whiskey, vinegar and sage. Place the meat in a large Ziplock bag and then pour in marinade and massage the marinade into the meat. Finish with black pepper and salt. Place in the fridge over night.

30 minutes before cooking remove the bag from the fridge and the meat from the bag. Allow the meat to get closer to room temp, which will help it cook faster.

Set your grill to very hot. Cooking flank steak is all about cooking fast and hot. Get a great sear on the steak and then heat to medium rare. Do not over cook your flank steak, it is not a forgiving cut of meat*. Once off the grill allow the steak to rest for five to ten minutes and slice into strips.

*If you like eating shoe leather then by all means over cook.

The Mushrooms: 10 Crimini mushrooms (quartered)

Olive oil

Sea salt

2 cloves Garlic

50 ML Beef stock

1/8th stick Butter.

Directions: In a pan on medium heat bring your oil to the point of smoke. Add garlic and brown your garlic. Add the mushrooms. If the garlic or mushrooms are getting too cooked, deglaze with beef stock. After about 10 minutes of sautéing add your butter and salt to taste. Let the butter melt in and take the pan off heat.

Double Green Puree: 2 Cups Sweet peas

1 cup Green onions (diced)

Olive oil

50 ML Rice wine vinegar

50 ML Lime juice

Pinch Red pepper flakes

Salt

Black pepper (cracked)

Butter

Directions: This puree is actually a play on the flavours of a mignonette. In an oiled pot on low to medium heat add your peas and green onion and begin to cook them down. As the mixture begins to brown a bit add your vinegar and lime juice and continue to cook until the peas begin to break down. Add your red pepper flakes and black pepper. Continue to cook until the mixture begins to really break down. Get your emersion blender and blend the contents of the pot while adding butter and salt to get a very creamy yet tangy/sweet flavour. As a composed dish the meat and mushrooms should give you lots of big meaty and earthy flavours while the puree is almost a palette cleanser. It gives the dish acidity, and some sweetness. The puree should also be a vibrant green colour which will pop beside the reddish meat and the brown mushrooms. It really brings a summery mood to the dish.

Thailand is the home of so much great food. Noodle dishes, grilled dishes, amazing seafood but what really brings the big flavours of Thailand is the curry.

Unlike Indian curry, Thai Curry is less of a heavy warming comfort food and more a thin consistency curry which adds fresh spicy kick to a Thai meal. Based on a totally unscientific survey of my friends Thai food seems to be much more popular than Indian cuisine, mostly because Indian food is too heavy and it's aromatics are unpleasant. While Thai cuisine is light and much more approachable. This I agree with in some ways but not in others.

Thai Cuisine has two divisive aspects that could turn off someone who is new, cilantro and spice. Cilantro also known as Green coriander or Mexican basil* actually tastes and smells bad to a significant section of the population because of genetic factors. The leafy herb gives of large amounts of a chemical group called aldehydes. Very similar compounds are released in soaps and in bedbugs. Most people's brains don't make the connection but there is a small amount of the population, who's brains do make their connection and thus Cilantro and many times Arugula taste unpleasant. Spice is the other one, many people prefer not to eat spicy food** but there is also many people who have legitimate health concerns when it comes to spicy food*** and that is understandable.

Some of the main ingredients in a Thai Curry are, coconut milk, lime, ginger, garlic, galangal****, onions, shallots, shrimp paste and lemongrass.

Here are a few common curries you will find in a Thai restaurant to make ordering a breeze. With this caveat, you need to communicate as much as you can with your server on how hot you can expect things. Heat is subjective, but sometimes just letting a server know you are sensitive to heat will allow them to communicate to the chef to tone down the heat. Or they may be sadist Buddhists who want to see you sweat (those are my favourite).

Kaeng Kari:(Yellow Curry) This curry is less yellow and more brown when it comes to you at the table. Normally this actually eats more like an Indian curry as it includes coriander, mace, cumin, fenugreek, garlic, bay leaf, and cinnamon. But there is also a Thai twist with the addition of lemongrass, galangal, palm syrup and coconut milk. Normally this is a medium heat curry but some places will ramp it up by adding ungodly amounts of chili.

Kaeng Khaio Wan:(Sweet Green Curry) This is where Thai cuisine really gets going with the interplay between sweet and heat. Green curries are super approachable because of their mellow flavour but many are made very hot as well. Normally served with chicken or shrimp this curry is a blend of kaffir lime, green chilies, galangal, white pepper, garlic, cumin seed, shrimp paste and fish sauce. The paste is then added to split coconut milk heated and served.

Massaman Curry:(Muslim Curry) Massaman Curry is a brown curry that plays with the sweet and spicy relationship. Easily my favourite curry because of its complexity and its hypocrisy. Nothing beats eating a "muslim" curry that is filled with crispy, tasty, BBQed pork and pork skin.*****   The Massaman Curry paste consists of coconut milk, tamarind syrup, roasted peanuts, potato, bay leaf, cardamom pods, star anise, cinnamon, chilies and fish sauce. It is also usually garnished with Thai Chilies which have been macerated in vinegar and palm sugar.

Phanaeng:(Penang Curry) Penang is a small island off the coast of Malaysia which is known as one of the great melting pots of Asian cuisine. This is a thai take on the much milder curry found on the island. It's a great beginner curry, because of it's mildness and it's ability to balance tropical flavours against usually beef cheek or flank steak.

Kaeng Phet:(Red Curry) If green means go, red mean stop. Red Curry is very similar to green curry but without that buffer of sweetness. The paste is essentially the same as a green curry but with the use of the hotter red Thai chili. Much less coconut milk is used and much more fish sauce. This curry was designed for beef, duck, pork, or frog, and it will make the undersides of your eye lids sweat.

Phat Phrik Khing:(Stir Fried Chili Ginger Curry) This is a dry curry that doesn't include coconut milk. It's very interesting in that it contains no ginger though its name would lead you to believe that it did. This is an oil based curry and if you are not a fan of coconut milk this may be the curry for you. Medium heat to high in spice, this curry is the flavours of thailand unadulterated. It's spicy, it's fresh, it's acidic but it's comforting.

So now that you have two types of curry under your belt(Indian, Thai) go out and explore what you like.

*The Mexicans are even taking basil's job.

**Pussies

***Ulcers, heart conditions, gastro-esophageal reflux, Crohn's & Colitis to name a few.

****An Indonesian root much like ginger but more pungent.

*****Sorry Islam

AUTUMN:

"...the air has that bracing autumnal bite so that all you want to do is bob for apples or hang a witch or something." - Sarah Vowell

There is no season as comfortable as the autumn for me and I want my fall food to speak to that theme of comfort.

Comfort food to some people tends to speak to a heaviness and in some ways it is true. Growing up the autumn was usually quite hot for at least it's first half an extended summer more than it truly being the fall. My fall food celebrates the tailgate, the beginning of red wine season, the warming effects of comforting soup.

Fall is waking up early on Sunday to cook for the football game. Huge pots of steaming chili, burgers, and other mystery meats encased in the innards of animals. It's big mugs of dark beer and congregation with friends in front of the big screen or at the tailgate before the big game.

Red wine season begins as the temperature drops, the colder it gets the richer the wine. There is nothing like short ribs braised in a big cabernet to signify the season.

Fall is also the season where scotch becomes a mainstay for me. Any time of the year one can enjoy a good single malt but when thing begin to cool down the cravings for that warming smokiness or malty richness become serious.

Fall is the season of one pot meals, packing as much as you can into your food getting ready for the long winter as the leave change and fall.

My fall food is about taking your time, developing big flavours, and warming your soul with a great hearty meal.

Foods You Should Know: Indian Curry

Curry is one of those words that immediately brings about a flood of sense memories. The aromatic spice, the richness, the heat, the vibrant colours, all come back to you when you hear that word. This is not saying that these memories are positive. North Americans seem to have a love hate relationship with curry and I plan to investigate why.

Curry is a generic term that westerners give to a large group of dishes from India, Sri Lanka, Pakistan, Afghanistan, Bangladesh, Thailand and other southeast asian countries. The word curry comes from the Tamil word "Kari" which essentially mean sauce. Generally, a curry is a dish with a mixture of spices which normally consist of a number of herbs and spices as well as chilies. They can be wet and soup or stew-like, or they can be dry. They can be fiery hot or creamy and rich.

Below I will talk about a few of the most popular curries in India which will make ordering at your local Indian Restaurant.*

Chicken Makhani(Butter Chicken): Butter chicken is training wheels for Indian food. It's mild in its heat and its flavour. There is nothing over the top butter chicken but it will really do a good job as an entry point to the flavours you will encounter in Indian cuisine. Butter, tomato paste, yogurt and spice marinated chicken, clove, cinnamon, ginger, garlic and fenugreek are all included in a classic butter chicken.

Korma: Korma is a general term for a curry with a think yogurt or cream based gravy or curry. Usually containing braised meats such as chicken, lamb, beef, or fish, korma is another great gateway curry. It's usually pretty mild when it comes to spice and flavour but it gives you a great idea of what a curry can be.

Tikka Masala: One of the great dishes of Great Britain. Most people will find this strange but for the historically illiterate readership, India was a British Colony for about 150 years. The Brits gave the Indians scotch and repressed emotions, and the Indians gave the Brits spices, grain and curry. Tikka Masala is now one of the great pub foods in Britain. It's mix of spice and huge flavours make it like a butter chicken on steroids, everything is amped up.

Saag: Saag is a spinach, mustard green and fenugreek green based curry that looks like a bizzaro creamed spinach. This Nepalese dish, is eating widely in northern India. It's usually spiced with star anise, clove, garam masala. It's light, super flavourful and usually pretty spicy. Usually made with lamb, paneer** or chicken.

Rogan Josh*:** This is a Kashmiri and Punjabi dish that is one of my favourites. Usually made with lamb, and a yogurt/browned onion/tomato based sauced. Usually much thinner in consistency than butter chicken or Tikka Masala, Rogan Josh blends the aromatics of clove, cinnamon, bay and cardamom with the heat of chilis. This is where things begin to get hot when it comes to this list.

Dhansak: Dhansak is a lentil curry that originates from Persia. It was brought to India but the Parsi people who were Zoroastrians**** exiled from what is modern day Iran. Lentils, vegetables, garlic, ginger and other garam masala based spices are braised with meat or squash to make a dry style curry which looks more like a mash of lentils and other reduced veggies reduced into a semi wet sauce. It's spicy and unbelievable filling.

Vindaloo: If you like spicy food this might be something you will be into. Either that or it will redefine spicy for you and you will bow to it as the pinnacle of foods that make the underside of your eyes sweat. Hailing from the Western coast of Middle India in the region of Goa, vindaloo is actually a hold over from the brief Portuguese occupation of India. Based on a wine and garlic dish from Portugal the people of Mumbai made this dish fiery hot hopefully as a park to the usually cruel Portuguese colonial rule. A blend of chili peppers, vinegar, ginger, and usually beef or chicken vindaloo will test your ability to handle spicy food.

Hopefully this gives you a bit of an overview of Indian cuisine and curry, the huge flavours and rich comforting nature of Indian cuisine makes it something that many people just need to try a few times before they really become fans of this cuisine. Starting with something like butter chicken or tikka masala is a great way to get into the flavours of Indian cuisine without stepping too far outside the box.

*Their curries will go from Mild to extremely Hot. Don't pee or touch your eyes after eating Vindaloo Curry.   Just a tip that I picked up from my penis.

**Paneer is an Indian farmers cheese that is almost rubbery but it also takes on the flavour of whatever it's cooked in.

***Lamb Rogan Josh is much more delicious than Joe Rogan Josh. But they both are great after a yoga class.

****Along with Rasputin, Karl Marx, and Confucius; Zoroaster sits on my Mount Rushmore for great beards in history.

*The Ghost Chili is the hottest chili in the world on the scoville scale with a rating between 300,000 and 1,000,000 units depending on it's cultivation and climate. To give you an idea tabasco sauce is about 5000-8000 scoville units. But the heat from the ghost chili is different. It really doesn't burn your tongue or really your mouth. It actually burns on the inside of you. Your body temp actually increases and you begin to sweat. Hot stuff on a hot day actually cools your body temp down in the long run because of the sweat. With that said if you want to use a less hot chili go for it but the flavour that comes with the heat of a ghost chili is transcendent. Safety tip: When working with these chilis wear gloves. The indian government has actually weaponized them, they are not a joke if you touch your eyes, nose, skin, genitals. Like seriously if you touch them and then go pee, you will have one of the worst 30 minutes of your life.

Curries are one of those comfort foods that people either love or hate. They can be creamy and savory or soupy and fiery hot or any number or derivations in between. This particular curry is rich and very hot. Usually on this blog I try to keep the heat level down so that you can adjust the spiciness to your taste, but in this case this curry needs to be hot or the flavours will not really make sense.

Ingredients:

2 Lamb shanks (bone In)

1 Large eggplant

1 can Chickpeas (strained and washed)

1 Large onion (rough chopped)

1 Star anise

2 tbs Turmeric

1 tbs Toasted cumin seed

1 tbs Toasted cardamom

1 tbs Toasted coriander

1 tsp Mustard powder

1 cup Lemon juice

1/2 cup Butter

1 Naga bhut jolokia pepper (ghost chili dried and flaked)*

1 liter Vegetable stock.

2 cups Basmati rice (cooked in rice cooker because I am lazy.)

Directions:

Pre heat your oven to 350. In a dutch oven add olive oil at high heat and sear the lamb shanks, this should only take about six or seven minutes. When the sear is on the meat remove meat from the container and place on paper towels. Drop heat to medium and add your onions and cook until they begin to char.** Then add your chick peas and eggplant and continue to stir them with the onions which are going to be dark brown/black. When thing begin to smoke add a little lemon juice to deglaze and reduce. Then add your spices and star anise(whole). Add more lemon juice and some veggie stock to cover all the ingredients, lower heat and simmer for 15 minutes. Return your lamb shanks to the dutch oven and add enough stock to submerge them. Cover and place in oven for 90 minutes.

**Usually I would not do this but with a curry it adds flavour depth if you burn your onions a bit. I know it seems counter intuitive but it really does make a gigantic difference.

Recipe Redux

Indian Cuisine and Wine is not an easy pairing. There is a school of thought that says an aromatic white like Gewurztraminer cools the mouth and has spice notes that compliment the Indian flavour profile which is fine but I like using a nice jammy Aussie Shiraz. Try out Schild Barossa Shiraz with this dish. With notes of black pepper, mint and eucalyptus and a jammy sweet berry front palate this wine pairs really well with the heat and the spice of this dish.

Foods You Should Know: Naan

There wasn't much I liked about living in Calgary for five years. Winters were shitty, the people are a little too well….Albertan for me.   One of those rare bright spots was the crash course I got in Indian Cuisine.

Calgary has one of the largest and most diverse Indian populations in North America. There cannot be a more opposite place climate wise for people from Indian to immigrate to. While I was a wine rep, the vast majority of the retailers I worked with were from somewhere in India. Hindus from Pradesh in the north, and Kerala in the south, Sikhs from Punjab, Muslims from Jammu and Kashmir along the Pakistani border, and Parsees from Mumbai made up much of the Indian immigrants whom with I worked.

Many days at work I ended up with three lunches because I was forcefully offered food by the store owners I worked with. Many of these family run liquor stores would have home cooked Indian food brought by family members in the back room.   I found nothing garnered more respect from these store owners than eating what was offered to you with no reservations*, and then asking what was in it. I looked down the barrel of a curry gun many times not know what it was loaded with. I had my first goat experience in the back room of a liquor store in northeast Calgary., I had a curry that made my eye lids sweat while sitting on a loading dock waiting for a shipment to arrive. And though I had had it many times before, I totally fell in love with Naan bread.

Naan is a generic term used to describe a leavened** flat bread found from the Middle East to as far south east as Thailand. Like Kim Chi in Korea, Dashi in Japan, or cheddar cheese in Wisconsin, Naan and it's unleavened cousin Roti is almost ubiquitous in India. Its part utensil, part sponge and all delicious.

Naan is traditionally cooked in a tandoor. A cylindrical clay and stone oven that burns wood or charcoal. These flat breads are flattened out and stuck to the inside wall of the oven and quickly cooked by the very high heats that are emitted. Most Naan are flavour with cumin seeds, saffron, butter and garlic. There is also another take on Naan known as Kulchas which are stuffed with all sorts of great stuff. If you are ever in downtown Calgary there is a restaurant called Moti Mahal, there food is great and affordable, but the star of that place is a Kulchas stuffed with Garlic and Paneer***. It's the definition of comfort food.

I find the best way to get into ethnic food is to find something that is familiar and go from there. There is nothing more familiar than bread. Naan is a great way to start introducing yourself to the vast flavour profile that India has to offer.

*Fuck, how much am I going to have to pay Anthony Bourdain for that one?

**Bread Science 101: Leavened bread is bread who's dough contains yeast or baking powder/soda which makes the dough rise. The yeast, eats sugars in the flour and releases carbon dioxide which makes the dough rise. When cooked these small pockets of Carbon Dioxide expand and you get more rising and a softening and stretching of the gluten molecules . Baking soda or powder does the same thing but through a different chemical reaction.   Naan is considered a flat bread but unlike most flat breads it is leavened so you get a light fluffy bread that can be crispy on the outside but silky and soft on the inside.

***Paneer is Indian farmers cheese. It's a tart and has almost a doughy consistency.

This is a medium difficulty recipe that pairs some of my favorite flavour profiles. Red wine braised beef and the southern french pairing of cumin and carrots. Also barley risotto just screams fall.

Ingredients: 4 Short ribs*

1.5 Cups California cabernet

Beef stock

1 tbs Cracked black peppercorns

1 Large onion (diced)

2 cloves Garlic (sliced)

2 Carrots (halved and rough chopped)

Canola oil

1 cup Pot barley (soaking in beef stock for about 30 minutes before cooking)

1/3 stick Butter

1 tbs Cumin

1 tsp Turmeric

Directions: In a large sauce pan on high heat, with canola oil, sear your short ribs** on all sides. I like to get my pan screaming hot for this, if you get a nice crust of caramelization on them. Bring the heat down to medium/low and add, your cracked black peppercorns, about 1/3 of your large diced onion and half of your sliced garlic. Continue to sauté this all together until your onions sweat (turn translucent and release their oils). Then add your wine, cover and let all those ingredients marry for about 10 minutes. After the ten minutes the wine will have reduced, add enough beef stock to cover your ribs and again cover and simmer for about an hour(stir and flip the ribs every so often). After the hour the ribs should be fork tender, carefully remove the ribs from the braising liquid(letting them rest on a cutting board), add about half of your butter, increase the heat and reduce by about half. ***

*You should go to a real butcher for these as I find super markets remove the cap of fat and connective tissue from their short ribs. This fat is what makes short ribs so tender and give you an amazing sauce.

**Liberally salting your ribs before they go in the pan is a great way to help with a crust.

***From here on out is your choice. I like to do a reduction of the braising liquid so that is what I am going to write. You can also make a roux and turn the braising liquids into a gravy. Both ways are acceptable, but I find that this dish is rich enough without throwing gravy on top of it.

****Barley is a great ingredient that doesn't really get its due when it comes to being a major component of a dish. It usually is an addition to a soup but I like to use it as a main carb in a dish.

*****The consistency of risotto will always be fought over by cooks. I will use Mario Batali's litmus test which is what I wrote above. Some people like it quite a bit thicker, do what you want. But know that if it's a gelatinous consistency you are wrong.

The Risotto:

Directions: In another sauce pan sweat the rest of your onions in canola oil. During that time in a bowl toss your carrots with some oil, salt, cumin and turmeric. Really get a nice coating on the carrots. You then add carrot, oil and spice mixture to the sauce pan. Increase heat to high and sauté until the carrots begin to get tender(5-7 minutes) You then add the Pot Barley**** and beef stock mixture to the sauce pan. Bring to a rolling boil for about four minutes, this will help release the starches from the barley and you will probably have to deglaze a bit with more stock. Don't be afraid to add stock, the barley will soak it up or the heat will evaporate it. You want to cook the barley down to tender, but with a little chalkiness in the middle.(just like doing risotto al dente.) The consistency of the risotto should be that when you scoop it onto your place the risotto spreads out and doesn't clump together. *****

Plating:

I like to put down the risotto first and then put the ribs on top. Then a healthy drizzle of the reduction over the ribs.

Recipe Redux

This seems like a simple pairing. You're cooking with Cabernet so why not drink a cabernet with the meal. I am going to go against that. Stags' Leap Petit Sirah will work well with the flavour profile. Petit Sirah is an inky black wine with big berry flavours and powdery tannins. It has a little more sweetness than most reds but it also has great tannic bitterness that gives the wine balance. The deep flavours of the braising liquid and the meat will work perfectly with this wine from the heart of Napa.

Foods You Should Know: Garlic

I hate the term "super foods" and every times my fingers strike the keys to create those words makes me cringe. Though if there was a food that deserves the title of super food it's garlic.

Garlic or allium sativum comes from the onion genus, closely related to shallots, leeks, onions, and chives. Garlic is a flowering bulb that produces flowers that are both male and female.*

Garlic originated in Central Asia but quickly spread East and West to China and Europe. Different sub species of garlic were developed in the ranging climates and soil types the vegetable spread to. Each of these species range in different sizes and flavours. Two different types of garlic emerged, Hard neck and Soft neck. There are five main varieties of hard neck and two varieties of Soft neck.**

In Europe there are actually several types of garlic which have protected geographical status. Like I have talked about in a few different articles in Braised Blue, Europe takes regionally very seriously. So seriously that they have made laws to protect the genetic purity of specific types of garlic grown in specific areas that are unique. These areas produce garlic that is distinct to the region and the regions cuisine. A few examples are:

Aglio di Voghiera from Emilia-Romagna in Northern Italy.

Ail blanc de Lomange from Lomange near Gascony, France.

Ail Rose de Lautrec from Lautrec in France

Ajo Morado de Les Pedroneras from Spain

Garlic is a versatile ingredient in many different cuisines around the world. Chinese cuisine uses garlic in many dishes and applications, as does Indian cuisine. In Asia, garlic in it's raw form is used for spice in dishes as well as a base flavouring component. Mediterranean cuisine is also very garlic heavy using garlic more as a base flavouring ingredient.

Garlic's flavour can range from very strong and distinct with a caustic burning nature in it's raw form to a much milder less aggressive garlics. The condition and freshness of the garlic also has a lot to do with the flavour. Just like an old onion, old garlic will be much more harsh and caustic. Most people who dislike garlic actually dislike garlic that isn't fresh because of how strong the aroma is. To tell if a bulb of garlic is fresh it's all about the colour and texture of the cloves. If the outer husk of the clove seems to be much bigger than the clove it's self you will most likely get a very strong flavoured garlic. If the garlic you buy is mushy or brown it's really not good and throw it out.***

Garlic has also been touted for it's many health benefits. It has natural broad spectrum antibiotic properties, meaning that it will inhibit the growth of infection in the body. It will not cure you but it will help give your immune system some backup. Garlic also has positive effects on high blood pressure, and heart disease. Garlic has also been shown to help anxiety and depression. In lab rats raw garlic has been shown to increase Seretonin levels in the brain which is a good tool in the fight against depression. The aromatherapy aspect of garlic is also great for anxiety.****

Overall, garlic is amazing it adds intense flavour to dishes from all over the world. Not everyone loves it but those who get it really do get it. Try and buy it as fresh as you can, don't use the jarred chopped shit*****. Slice it thin, fine and use it liberally.

*Yup, that's right Garlic is the official vegetable of hermaphrodites.

**Hardneck: Porcelain, Purple Striped, Marble Purple Stripes, and Glazed Purple Striped, and Rocambole. Softneck: Artichoke and Silverskin

***I feel as though if 21 year old me read this I would thank me because I have eaten some bad garlic in the past. It's not pleasant.

****Think of people who believe wearing a necklace of garlic to bed to deter vampires. It's a silly superstition which is grounded in some truth. If you are a person who is afraid of vampires to the point of losing sleep, the scent of garlic will help to stem that anxiety. No matter how batshit nuts you are.

*****I know everyone has the chopped garlic in oil in their fridge and it's easy just to dump into a dish. Just remember garlic does go bad even if it's sitting in oil for months or years on a store shelf. Is there a chance that maybe you've never had real fresh high quality garlic if this is the junk you've been using? The answer is yes.

I've done other cedar plank salmon recipes on Braised Blue but this one is a little bit different because it creates more of a candied salmon effect. If you're not a fan of sweetness going with your fish or meat it may not be up your alley, but I have created this recipe as a great way to cover up a maybe not super fresh piece of salmon(not "gone bad" just not fresh). The glaze also really does a great job in blending heat with sweet which is something I am a huge fan of.

Ingredients:

1 fillet Salmon

1 Cedar plank (soaked for 12 hours)

2/3 cup Maple syrup

1/3 cup Sriracha sauce

1 tsp Crushed red chilis

Sea salt

Black pepper

Recipe Redux

This dish has many of layers of flavour which makes it a little difficult to pair with a wine. Between the balance between heat and sweetness, crispy chewy caramelization and tender moist fish, there is an underlying flavour of smoke that I feel screams for a match. This is why I am going to break from my self imposed ban on recommending Canadian wines just for today. Road 13 Vineyards out of Oliver B.C. makes a Syrah that is equal parts smokey, barnyardy and really nicely acidic. It's rare for me to give a Canadian wine this much credit but it also comes in around $20 a bottle which isn't terrible. Sometimes when you are choosing a wine for a dish playing it against an undertone vs. playing it against the upfront flavours can lead to really great results.

Directions: Take your pre-soaked cedar board and lay your salmon on it. In a mixing bowl add your maple syrup, sriracha, chilies, salt and pepper and mix. The sauce should be thick and sticky. Then using a silicon brush, paint the fish with the sauce. Place in a BBQ preheated to around 350 degrees and begin to cedar smoke the salmon. Every few minutes apply a new layer of the sauce. It should quickly form a crust on the outside of the fish. This crust keeps the moisture in the fish while creating a crunchy surface. The fish should be smoked/ cooked for about 45 minutes to an hour, while you continue to apply the sauce every few minutes.

This can be served whole as a protein in a dish. Or shredded up in a salad or on a sandwich. It's just a great recipe if you have extra salmon or some salmon which isn't super fresh. Enjoy!

In Vino Veritas: Learn A Little, Drink Better, Drink Less

There is a large part of the wine drinking public who takes great pride in claiming they know nothing about wine, and that it all tastes the same to them.   I am not for eugenics in many cases but I will add this one to the list.

Where does this mindset come from? Is it born of pure frugality? The ability to grit your teeth through stemmy swill and lie to yourself about how ambivalent you are about wine as a whole isn't something to be proud of.   I am all for finding an inexpensive wine to drink with dinner but I also want something really good.

As I talked about in an earlier In Vino Veritas, people buy wine for lots of reasons that have nothing to do with the actual wine. A cute label or a memorable name is an understandable reason to purchase a wine. It's years of psychological marketing laser guided to your brain to maximize the chance that you will choose their product.

My goal in this piece is three fold. I want you to learn a little about where the value is in wine. I want you to spend a little bit more on your wine and in turn you will probably drink less and save yourself the money in the long run.* I hit the point in my life where if I was going to drink and brave a hangover the next morning, I was going to make it worth my while. Here are four wines priced under $20.

1. Beringer Founders Estate Cabernet Sauvignon: North Coast California: Bright, full, round berry fruit, powder tannins and it's all for about $18. I love this one because it really lingers flavour wise but it's not jammy and sweet.

2. Stoneleigh Sauvignon Blanc: Marlborough, New Zealand: A clean, easy drinking white with lots of grassy notes paired with a nice grapefruit punch. The finish is gooseberry but it's short and sweet(not literally). Great acid but nothing overbearing.

3. Rocca Della Macie Chianti Classico Riserva: Chianti Classico, Tuscany, Italy: A bright acid punch upfront belies how delicate this wine is. A floral nose of rose petals and game meat** works well with a palate of red fruit, truffle and rubber. For $15 you cannot beat the value on this one.

4. El Hada Verdejo: Rueda, Spain: Verdejo is one of my favourite white variety. It has great acid but also really interesting fruit combinations. El Hada has a nose of orange blossom which is so pungent and perfumed it will blow your mind. The flavours in the wine begin with grassy and fade into lime and other citrus fruit. Unlike Stoneleigh this wine is medium to full bodied. The acidity creates almost a creamy mouthfeel but at the same time clean. The perfect patio wine. This one comes into at around $17 or $18.

So you now have no excuse to buy Barefoot or Naked Grape again. You have four news ones to try. I suggest you expand your horizons.

*Here is my sneaky footnote where I say if you still drink wine only to get drunk, stop reading this right now. Go buy some Tequiza, drink it in the bath tub and puke in your soap dish. This piece is not for you, and you probably find this book insulting on a bunch of levels but if that works for you, I guess keep reading.

**Yes this sound very strange but it works.

This isn't some crazy elaborate meal. This is a side dish that anyone can do on the BBQ or in the oven it takes half an hour and you will have your mind blow by how good it is and how little you had to do.

Ingredients:

2 Russet potatoes (sliced into 1/2 inch pieces)*

2 Leeks (washed and sliced thin)

2 cloves Garlic

Sea salt

Pepper

Grape seed oil

1 tbs Butter.

Directions:

In a mixing bowl add all of your ingredients and except for the butter. Add enough oil to coat everything liberally. Hand mix everything get the oil, salt and pepper distributed. Then take a large piece of aluminum foil (two feet or so) and pour the contents onto the foil. Add the butter and wrap the contents tightly in the foil.** In an oven set at 400 degrees, put the package on a baking sheet and cook for about 30 minutes. On a barbecue again at around 400 degrees put the package on the top rack, (which is the hottest part of the grill when you keep the top closed. I repeat, when you keep the top closed. Again 30 minutes of cooking will have these potatoes, leeks and garlic nice and caramelized.

This is the perfect super easy side dish that can go with so many things. The leeks give the potatoes a smokey flavour that you just don't get with onions. I love doing this side dish with steak as you can just put the potatoes on while you preheat the grill. Give it a try.

*Take two chopsticks and put them at the sides of the potato length wise. These will allow you to cut into the potato but not all the way through which will fan out the potato and allow the butter to soak in without just pooling in the foil. Also quickly rinsing the potato after cutting will wash away some starch and keep the potato from sticking together.

**I've seen cooking shows call this a hobo pouch. In my next book I will teach you how to heat beans in a can and how to properly fold a bindle.

The Angel's Share: A Not So Brief Introduction To Scotch.

In my time in Calgary I worked for two years overseeing the largest retail single malt scotch collection in Canada. My time with this retailer wasn't always positive and my exit from the company was even less positive. However this two years of selling and buying for such an amazing collection puts me in a position where I should be doing a weekly scotch column for someone*. So here is my tryout. In the next 1200 or so words I am going to give you a crash course on scotch.

What is scotch?

Scotch is a whiskey, which has been produced, aged and bottled in Scotland. But this is just scratching the surface. Scotch Whisky actually can be broken down into three sub classifications which have their own rules.

Blended Scotch Whisky: This is whisky which contains a blend of **malt** based spirit and non-malt based spirit. This blending process allows for a consistent product. ex. The Johnny Walker Line(minus Green label), Ballantines, Chivas, White and McCay, Bells, Dewars.

Blended Malt Scotch Whisky: This is similar to blended scotch whiskey except for that 100% of the spirit in the bottle is from malted barley. At this point in time the real whiskey mavericks and risk takers occupy this realm. You will see these whiskies less frequently because they are usually made as limited edition products by smaller productions known as **independent bottlers**. Ex, Johnny Walker Green Label, The Compass Box Series, Smokehead, Premium Bottlers.

Single Malt Whisky: Single Malt Whiskey is the most renown the three classifications. Whiskies with this classification must be made from 100% barley malt, they must be batch produced in a pot still, and all of the spirit in the bottle must be from the same distillery. Single malts are inherently inconsistent though there are practices that allow distillers to create consistent product.

Does The Age Of My Scotch Matter?

Yes and No. The age statement is actually sort of an interesting system. First off the age of a whisky is the time it stays in the barrel. If you have 20 years in a barrel and 20 in a bottle the whisky is still only 20 years old.

First, you don't have to put an age statement on your bottle, it's 100% voluntary. It actually is more of a marketing tool/guideline for the buyer than an precise statement. The age statement only denotes the age of the youngest whiskey in the bottle. A bottle of Glenlivet 12 may have 30 year old whisky in it to give specific characteristics to the flavour profile, but because the youngest whisky in the bottle is 12 years old, the age statement is 12. If you look at Glenmorangie they do not put an age statement on their four lowest priced whisky. This allows them to blend to a specific style and flavour profile without being tied to an age statement.

Second, it's a personal taste thing. I personally like a younger whisky, they are more robust and lively on the palette, their cost is lower and young whisky tends to exhibit a little more in your face flavour. Older Whisky is more subtle, it's heavier on the palette and there is less burn. The flavours are more complex and developed but there is little vibrancy or liveliness.

What does Highland Mean?

There are five distinct regional classifications for single malt whisky. Though the system can be a little convoluted and geographically eyebrow raising.

Lowland Whisky: Lowland whisky is any whisky distilled south of Glasgow. There are only four lowland distilleries still in production. Girvan, Auchentoshan**, Glenkinchie, and Bladnoch. Generally lowland whisky is lighter in flavour with floral or citrus notes. Auchentoshan is actually known as breakfast whisky by connoisseurs because it is triple distilled and drinks much too easy to drink after the noon hour. I would recommend Auchentoshan 12 as a great place to start when it comes to getting into scotch. It comes in around $50 a bottle and it is approachable but also complex.

Highland Whisky: Highland Whisky is where things go off the rails. The highland region comprises anything north of Glasgow with the exception of the Island of Islay and the Mull of Kintyre. The highland region also has a sub region which comprises the islands not named Islay. The Island sub region covers the isles of Arran, Mull, Jura, Orkney, and Skye. To complicate matters, there is no real flavour profile that comprises highland whisky, or island whisky. They run the gamete of flavour profiles. A few examples of these are: *Highland: Oban, Glenmorangie, Dalwinnie, Dalmore, Tullibardine, Royal Lochnagar. Island: Scapa, Highland Park, The Arrans Malt, Isle Of Jura, Tobermory, Talisker,*

Speyside Whisky: Speyside Whisky is any distiller which draws water from the river Spey or any of its tributaries. The largest concentration of distilleries in Scotland are centered in this small area. Like the highland region there isn't really a distinct flavour profile that governs the area. Ex. Craggenmore, Glenfiddich, Glendronach, Glenlivet, The Macallan, Balvenie, Linkwood, Longmorn, Aberlour, Benriach

Islay Whisky: First and foremost Islay is pronounced (Eye-Lah), not (IS-LAY), not (I-Lay) Whiskies from Islay are generally very peaty. The one exception to this is Bruichladdie which comes in peated and unpeated varieties. Ex. Lagavulin, Laphroig, Bruichladdie, Port Charlotte, Ardbeg, Bowmore, Kilchomen, and Bunnhabhain.***

Campbeltown Whisky: Campbeltown is a small town on the very tip of the Mull of Kintyre**** A few hundred years ago, Campbeltown has the most unlicensed distilleries per capita in Scotland. Distilling was a family past time and keeping it off the books was the best fuck you to the English they could think of. Nowadays Campbeltown has three functioning, on the books distilleries. Springbank, Glengyle, and Glen Scotia. Campbeltown whiskies are known for being intense, well balanced whiskies. Springbank is probably my overall favourite single malt.

What Kind of Scotch Should I Buy For Myself?

Well it really is all about what you like, it's the beauty of single malt. There are hundreds of different flavour profiles to explore. When I advised customers who were just starting out I did my best to find them something lighter. Laphroig is going to scare off even a seasoned highland drinker. I would recommend Auchentoshan 12 because of its price point, its value and its lighter style.   Longmorn would be another favourite, it's a big powerful spirit but it has much sweeter notes than similar whiskies. Kind of a creme brûlée thing going on. And third would be Glenrothes, they have different vintages which gives you an idea of how variable scotch can be year to year, but it is all very approachable stuff at the same time.

Glossary:

Malt: Any grain can be malted, but in scotch whisky it only refers to barley. Malting is the act of drying out germinated cereal grains. It's one of the primary steps of alcohol production.

Independent Bottlers: This is a company that buys already distilled spirit by the barrel from single malt distillers. They exist as a means of cash flow for many of the smaller distilleries in Scotland. Ex. AD Ratray, Gordon MacPhail.

Marrying Whiskey:Because the word Blending denotes a different product the term marrying is applied to the mixing of different whiskies produced in the same distillery. Your 15 year old whisky probably has 18-20-21-and 30 year old whisky in it.

Peat: A mossy biofuel used in the drying process of the germinated barley. Peaty scotches smell and taste smokey depending on how long and how intense the drying process is. Peat can be expressed in different ways. From smokey, to briny, to iodine-like flavours.

Cask Strength: This is a whisky that is not diluted before bottling. These whiskies can get as powerful as 60% alcohol but they are an awesome value because you can dilute to your taste and really stretch out the bottle.

The Angel's Share: During the aging process, some of the spirit in the barrels will evaporate. This small amount of volume lost is known as The Angel's Share.

Chill Filtration: This is a process before bottling where the whisky is cooled until the oils separate. They are then skimmed off which makes your whiskey not cloud when ice or cold water is added. It's also a great way to remove flavour and mouthfeel from your whisky.

*And who knows maybe getting paid for it....hint hint.

**Auchentoshan is known by many Scots as dessert whisky or breakfast whisky depending on the depth of the alcohol problem of the particular Scot.

***I would like to say that I not only remembered all the Islay distilleries but I also spelled them correctly by memory.

****AKA Scotland's Wang

Blogs are inherently self indulgent but good blogs are not too self indulgent so I will just give you guys an awesome recipe for a soup since it's bloody cold out today.

This is a super easy recipe that you don't really need to do a ton of work on. It's kind of a great soup to throw into a slow cooker and leave on its own all day. You can even make this an easier recipe by going to your local super market, buying a roasted chicken pre made and using the chicken for the soup(if you are running short on time). What's great in this is the amount of half and half used it pretty small for how creamy the soup will be. This is done with the use of the russet potato which will release it's starch and give the soup more body without the need for lots of dairy.

Ingredients:

1 Onion (diced)

5 Chicken thighs (cooked and shredded) or 3 Cups of Pre-Cooked rotisserie chicken.

2 Heads Corn on the cob*

1 Poblano pepper** (cut into thin strips)

1.5 cups Monterey jack cheese (shredded)

1 clove Garlic (finely diced)

1 medium Russet potato (diced)

1 Cup of Half and half

4 Cups of Chicken stock

1 tbs Cumin

Sea Salt

Black pepper

1 tbs Chili powder

*For best effect put on your coat and cook them on the BBQ to get some nice char on the corn, then cut the corn off the cob. It will bring a huge amount of depth of flavour to the soup. Mind you it's cold out so this really depends how badly you want to suffer for your soup.

**For best effect blister the pepper on a grill, removed the skin and deseed/remove the core.

Directions:

In a large pot or slow cooker add your onions and sweat them until translucent, then add your garlic. Then add your chicken and corn along with your spices. Add your potatoes and allow them to release their starch and take on the flavours of the contents of the pot. Then add your stock and bring to a boil while stirring. Add your half and half and bring the heat down to a simmer. Simmer the soup for as long as needed but no less than 90 minutes. This will integrate the flavours as well as reduce the soup down a bit. The soup should be a thicker texture like a normal clam chowder so reduce or add stock as needed.

Serving: Ladle your soup into bowls and top with the roasted poblanos(which have been in the fridge) and shredded cheese. This will add a cool yet spicy element to the hot soup. It's a very interesting play on temperature as well as spice.

Recipe Redux:

I am not the kind of guy who pairs wine with soup. It's a weird flavour issue that I could never wrap my head around. However I do like beer with soup. This soup really works well with a nice IPA, Red Racer IPA is from Surrey British Columbia, and it arguably one of the only things worth a damn ever to leave Surrey. This includes professional wrestler Rick Bognar who's claim to fame was being the second Razor Ramon in the WWF after Scott Hall drank himself out of the "sport".

Since I was about 20 I've been making chili. It was one of the first dishes I learned to make and in university* it was a crowd pleaser that you could eat for an entire week if you made enough of it. Over the past decade I have evolved this recipe. I don't think I've ever made it the same twice but I may mention something about the meat in the chili once or twice. It is not a classic chili by any means; It has beans, it's spicy, it has two different meats in it, it is sweet, and it should be cooked in a pot. This is not a pour everything into a slow cooker and coming back in 2 hours kind of a chili. This is a three to four hour job and the first 45 minutes of it is about treating the meat in the best possible way. Chili is about the meat, the other flavours, textures and consistencies are where you play jazz. As long as your meat is done properly the rest of the dish is about being patient and layering the flavours. As you will see, I am serious about this, it's not an easy recipe.

Ingredients:

1.5 lbs of Ground bison brisket

3 Chorizo sausages** (casings removed and the meat hand shredded)

1 bottle Willy's chili sauce***

2 Cloves Garlic (rough chopped.)

1 Can of Black beans.

1 dried Ancho chili (cut into strips)

3 Roma tomatoes (rough chopped)

4 Poblano peppers (rough chopped)

2 Thai chilies (diced)

1 tbs Cumin

1 tbs Smoked paprika

Open a bottle of your favorite dark ale****

*The residents of 38 Wanda Rd were my beta testers for this recipe during one of our many, "bring your own defibrillator nights". These nights would end with pants unbuttoned and left arms tingling.

**You need real chorizos not processed filler added sausages. These babies need to be pulled apart and shredded into ground beef consistency.

***This is a total cop out. It is just that I don't expect you to pickle your own peppers. Willy's is a chili sauce with pickled peppers in it. It's a no fuss way to get the acidity and some sweetness into the chili. You can get it at Zehers.

****And 11 of it's friends should be chilling to pair with this chili.

Directions:

The Meat: In a large deep pot, with a little canola oil, on medium high heat.**** Brown the shredded chorizo. Then add the bison by pinching the meat off into small chunks and continue to brown all of the meat. You want to get a nice amount of char on the chunks of bison, they are going to act like mini meat balls that will get a nice crust when it's dropped into the put full of the fat from the chorizo. Remember do not dice up the meat with your flipper you want chunks of bison. If you need to, and you probably will, deglaze the pot with beer, it's just a nice way to cool the pot down and pick up all those meaty flavours off the surface of the pot and back into the meat, this is the base of the entire dish, making sure you are creating big meaty flavours.***** When the meat is cooked bring your temp down to medium/low you add the dried Ancho chili, let the pepper soak up that meat base and release it's flavours. Continue to de-glaze if needed. You then add the cumin and paprika mix it all together with the meat base. You then add the Thai chili. And you meat should be done after about 45 minutes you want the meat sitting in this rich smokey stew like concoction.

The Rest: Add the beans first, they will soak up the beefy sauce and kind of act like floating meat distribution systems while the chili cooks. You then add the tomato. You then add the chili sauce, I usually add half the bottle and leave half in case I feel I need to give more of the acidity and sweetness. Add to your taste. You then turn down to low heat, cover and let those flavours marry for about 3 hours. I like to stir every 10 minutes just to make sure nothing sticks to the bottom. At low heat it shouldn't really happen unless you really neglect it. With about 15 minutes left to go add the diced poblano peppers but save some for garnish. They will bring some bright fresh flavours to the chili. Also as you stir taste the chili, make sure everything is in balance. There should be a smokey meaty undertone to the chili the heat should not be over powering.****** There should be some sweetness as well, I like to balance sweet against heat. The consistency of the chili should not be watery but your spoon should not be able to stand up the in the pot. Somewhere in between, to your taste. I like to top the chili with a little bit of shredded Colby cheese (cheddar will do) diced poblano peppers and cilantro.

Eating Instructions: You should eat this with a stick of French bread in one hand and a spoon in the other.******

Writer's Note I would like to gloat that I made this chili in 2013 with pork tongue sausage instead of chorizo and won a chili cookoff against 6 other chilies. Sorry Alex, Palmer, Amy Kidd, Bryson Parks, Dr. Kielbasa, and Dan "Jones" Algar this is my victory dance.

*****I used a 10.5 liter stock pot and by no means do i fill it but it's a lot of surface area to a whole lot of meat more evenly.

******You will also want to make sure you meat is chunky. I almost pinch off the meat and compress it.

*******My friend and noted playwright David W. Ouellette and I made a habanero chili that made us both feel like we had appendicitis. It was the most manly moment followed by the least manly moment of my life.

********This means you are really going to get inventive when you are drinking those beers I mentioned in footnote number three.

Foods You Should Know: Maple Syrup

There is nothing more Canadian than Maple syrup.

This distinctly sweet substance has been a mainstay in canadian cuisine for hundreds of years. Most people know generally how it is obtained and processed but is Canada selling its self short when it comes to how it brings this product to market?

Maple Syrup is the processed product that comes from the sap of the sugar maple, black maple and red maple trees. These trees are found all over Eastern Canada, and New England, but in the biggest concentration in Quebec in the foothills of the Laurentian Mountains. Quebec actually produces three quarters of the maple syrup in the world.

The production of maple syrup was a skill learned by early Canadian settlers from the native people of Quebec. Like many other organisms trees synthesize and store sugar as an energy source, this sugar is called sap. Maple trees happen to produce more sap than the average tree. During the spring the maple tree usually has excess sap that can be tapped by cutting into the tree. This sap is then collected, and taken for processing.*

Processing is simple but also an art. The sap is boiled and the excess water in the sap is evaporated. This is an extremely delicate process, if the sap is under boiled it will come out watery and can spoil easily, if it is over cooked it begins to crystallize.** Knowing when to stop the boil is part science and part experience. Usually a hydrometer is used to measure the brix (residual sugar) but the colour is also a determining factor, because the classification system used by the Canadian Food Inspection Agency (CFIA).

The colour of maple syrup has to do with its sugar concentration, the longer a producer cooks the sap down the darker and more caramelized the sugar will become. CFIA has a three tiered rating system which denotes the colour of the syrup. Level 1 is comprised of extra light, light and medium, Level 2 is amber, and Level 3 is dark. Seems simple enough right? Maybe a little bit too simple.

In the past year the Canadian Federal Government passed legislation which banned products like Aunt Jemima from calling themselves "Maple Syrup" though they could just label themselves as "Maple Flavoured Syrup" which most consumers wouldn't notice or care about. This is why I, as well as many others, would like to see a system of classification which clearly denotes the origin and quality level of Canadian Maple Syrup and gives Maple Syrup Producers the right to seek restitution from large companies essentially selling sugar and chemicals while using the words "Maple" and "Syrup" to give their swill legitimacy.

Much like the DOC systems in Italy or the AOC systems in France, Canadian Maple Syrup Producers and the government should make Maple Syrup a distinctly regional Canadian product. This will keep quality high, and allow those who really do produce a great product the ability to differentiate themselves from the fakers and also take the fakers to task legally.

*A mature sugar maple can produce about 40-55 Litres of sap per year. But it takes about 30 litres of sap to produce 1 litre of Maple Syrup. This means only about 1.5 litres of syrup per tree is produced.

**Maple Sugar is the result of this which to be honest is a mighty tasty mistake.

I have always found most butternut squash soups pretty disappointing. They are smooth, and mild but they don't really offer much more than that. I have made some changes to the classic butternut squash soup while at the same time making it sound much more ominous. In a previous article I talked about Naga Bhut Jolokia peppers, also known as the ghost chili. These are when dried and cured properly the hottest peppers in the world. This recipe is not for the faint of heart, it is over the top spicy but with that spice comes balance in the texture of the soup and in the sweetness. You have been warned.*

Ingredients:

1 Butternut squash (broken down, deseeded,)

1 large Onion (diced)

2 cloves Garlic (diced)

Vegetable stock

Grape seed oil

1 cup Maple syrup

1 Naga bhut jolokia pepper (remove about 50% of the seeds.)

1/2 cup Butter.

Cinnamon

Cumin

Coriander

Cardamom

Black pepper

Sea salt**

*If you cannot find ghost chilies or you do have a faint heart some chipotles will work as well but just know that I have a disappointed facial expression directed at you.

**Keep in mind that this is vegetarian and it's coming from me so please be impressed.

Directions:

In a large pot, on medium heat with grape seed oil, sweat your onions. Add your garlic as the onions begin to go brown. You actually want to caramelize the onions to the point where they begin to char. This is an Indian technique to create a different depth of flavour in the dish. You then deglaze with a little but of vegetable stock. Add your butternut squash, black pepper, cardamom, coriander, cumin and cinnamon. This step should take about 15 minutes of just heating and stirring making sure the squash begins to soften up. You then add your ghost chili and continue to sauté, deglaze with the vegetable stock when needed. You then add your maple syrup and continue to sauté. After about 10 more minutes add stock until the contents of the pot are submerged. Put the heat down to simmer, cover, and go watch an episode of Person of Interest or some shit. After about 45 minutes you need to use your handy dandy emersion blender but before that add that butter. You want a silky smooth consistency to the soup so making sure you blend at the surface of the soup will ensure you inject enough air into the soup.***
No to top this soup I recommend topping it with some grated gruyere cheese and some chopped scallions.

***TAKE THE SOUP OFF OF HEAT BEFORE YOU IMMERSION BLEND!!! It will save you third degree burns.

Recipe Redux:

Again I am going to pair a beer with a soup, this time I am going with Unibroue's La Fin Du Monde. This Trappist style ale from Quebec has a flavour profile which will match well with the spices in this soup and the high alcohol content will help in a big way to cool the mouth. This beer may translate to "the end of the world" but it's a super easy drinking Belgian style beer with huge flavours of citrus and coriander spice. This is some of my favourite beer from Canada and it doesn't nearly get the respect it is due.

In Vino Veritas: Red Wine Season Is Upon Us

Many people don't realize the seasonality of wine. Because it sits on a shelf at the liquor store all year long we don't really see the market trends or the human behavior behind those trends.

Wine was believed to be produced as early as 7000 BCE in what is now known as The Republic of Georgia in South Eastern Europe. By 4500 BCE we see small scale wine production throughout the Mediterranean. The ancient Greek, Egyptian and Roman Empires upped the ante when it comes to wine production. Growing populations and a move to cities meant that wine production needed to be organized. During these periods we see an evolution from clay pots made to hold wine, to barrels made to transport wine over long trips. During this period we see gods and deities devoted to wine, promoting its ritual consumption during festivals of fertility. In the ancient world, wine meant sex and sex meant children*(Cue The Circle of Life sung by Billy Joel.).

The newly formed Roman Catholic Church saw this relationship between wine and fertility. They co-opted the use of wine in ritual from the pagans**, it was such a successful practice that exists to this day. In the Catholic Church and a few other older Christian sects it is believed that, wine is literally transformed into the blood of Christ by these rituals***. Those are some powerful grapes.

In the business of wine there are cycles that follow the seasons as well. Starting in October for Thanksgiving and going to april or so, the consumption of red wine is at its highest. These seven months comprise about 80% of the red wine sales in Canada. Of course this normally coincides with the holiday season but it also has to do with weather. Red wine pairs with cold weather just as well as it pairs with beef.

It is more than just the weather. Human beings for now thousands of years have had a relationship with wine. There is a scientific field called ethnobotany which studies the relationship between plants and human culture. Famed counter culture writer and thinker Terrance McKenna in his book *Food of The Gods: The Search for The Original Tree of Knowledge. A Radical History of Plants, Drugs and Human Evolution****,* surmised that human beings have evolved on a parallel with the plants they happened to coincide with. McKenna believes that the longer that human culture is in contact with a plant or substance, the more engrained it becomes in our culture. From what we can gather wine has been around for nearly 9,000 years this cultural impression is remarkable.

It can be assumed that we drink more wine starting in about October because it is the natural time between harvest of the grapes, their processing, fermentation and distribution. For millennia, a fresh batch of wine would have been ready to drink in October, as the days get shorter and food hopefully is plentiful enough to get through the winter. People would celebrate the Equinox with drinking and revelry and as the year moved on the Winter Solstice was another wine centric event. Human beings today seem to follow this ancient cue to begin drinking more wine.

Most wine companies spend the vast majority of their sales budgets during the "holiday season" or OND(October, November, December). And one could argue that the entire retail sector values these months most but in the liquor industry you really do see a change in customer behavior during these months. Customers are more willing to spend money on a bottle of wine for dinner today than they were two months ago. This is a fact, it is engrained in our collective unconscious to drink either more or better.

I guess this aimless history lesson needs a point. That point is that wine is not just a packaged good, it's a substance we have evolved with a substance that has influenced how we live our lives and a product that mirrors us in a way*****. So eat, drink and enjoy the season.

*Take a look about 9 months from the Shores of Erie Wine Festival(June) and see how many people are having children. There may be a not so odd bump in the birth rate.

**We see the early Roman Catholic Church take on several concepts from pagan belief systems to make Christianity more palatable for new Catholics. Another example of this was the worship of the Virgin Mary. Because many pagan belief systems included and at times featured female deities, the familiarity of The Virgin Mary became a powerful draw for the Church during it's expansion.

***Christ's blood has a faint aroma of violets, it's much better than Christ's blood last week. It's was a little too barnyardy for my liking.

****Yes I know this is the longest bloody book title ever. But the book is really great when it comes to outlining the social history of wine, coffee, sugar, tea, cannabis, hallucinogenic mushrooms and other plants and drugs.

*****I also wanted to make jokes about Billy Joel's alcoholism, accidental pregnancy, the bouquet of Christ's blood and the Catholic Church.

The Angel's Share" More Expensive Then Drugs

One of the biggest reasons why people don't get into scotch is the price. It's a luxury item but it is by no means a ripoff.

Even at its most mechanized and automated the production of single malt whiskey is a painstaking and time consuming process that in my opinion earns it's price tag. What this piece aims to do is talk about the process of single malt production in a little more depth than most articles will. I also want to deter people from ever buying an expensive vodka ever again.

How Single Malt Is Made:

I am going to keep this as simple as I can while trying to add some colour at the same time.

There are five main processes that go into the production of single malt whisky.

Malting:

Barley is purchased from local farmers or grown by the distillery itself. The barley is steeped in water and laid out on a malting floor. Think of a hockey arena sized room without the ice. The wet barley will begin to germinate(sprout) the barley is then manually turned by fire hydrant shaped men named Colin or Padraig. This turning manual turning and built in quality control regulates how much oxygen and temperature the germinating barley comes into contact with.

The process of germination begins to release sugars from the grain these sugars are what sweet sweet alcohol comes from. At the precise time the germination must be arrested as the barley will begin to use the sugars for sustenance and we want those sugars.

The germination is arrested by a kilning process. In traditional floor malting the floor is actually part of the kiln. The sprouted barley is dried by the heat and smoke of the kiln. Depending on whether or not you want a peated whisky the fuel for the kiln is either coal, natural gas or peat moss. Peat Moss releases a pungent, earthy smoke that clings to the wet barley and becomes integrated with the grain. Coal and Natural gas do not impart flavour.

After the dried barley is allowed to naturally cool for up to six weeks it is then milled. The barley is crushed usually in large industrial milling machines into a coarse oatmeal like substance called Grist. The big part of the milling is removing the outer husk of the barley and exposing the sugary inside this makes the next step a much more efficient process.

Mashing:

Once the grist is ground up the process of mashing takes place. In a large vat called a mash tun the grist is mixed with hot water. The water begins to dissolve the sugars and separates the husks which float more readily. What you get is a sweet almost milky solution called wirt. There is normally three washings of the grist and the each time the wirt is drained off and reserved.* Once you get a concentrated wirt with enough sugar your next step is fermentation.

Fermentation:

Fermented barley is essentially beer. So you can say that whisky makers are also brewers. A high quality whisky comes from a high quality fermentation of barley.

So how do we make beer? Well, we have wirt, this sugary chunky solution, that needs to go hang out with a proprietary blend of yeasts**. Some of these yeast blends are hundreds of years old and kept under lock and key in labs. At first the yeast reproduces in the wirt creating almost a film over the liquid. This film creates a barrier which protects the mixture from oxygen. When oxygen starved the yeast begins to take the sugars in the solution and convert them to alcohol and carbon dioxide. This phase is very important because of the rapid production of alcohol. This is also when the solution is at its least stable, climate inside the fermenter and the building must be maintained as any large fluctuations can ruin the process. When the alcohol level rises to an acceptable point the fermented wirt is then cooled and the yeast quickly dies. You now have a beer like substance that tastes more like a beer milkshake.***

Distillation:

Simply put, distillation is the physical process of separating mixtures based on the different volatilities of components of the mixture through boiling.(maybe that wasn't so simple)

The important part of this is that a pot still can only make one batch of spirit at a time. In single malt production it is laid out by law that a pot still must be used, this style of still is much less efficient but it also allows the distiller to control the process with much more precision. The use of copper for the pot is two fold. Copper is one of the best materials when it comes to the conduction of heat, and there are compounds in copper which bind to compounds in the distilling mixture. These compounds are impurities which can impart bitterness or metallic flavours to the spirit.

As the beer like mixture heats in the pot area of the still. Alcohol is the first compound to evaporate. This alcohol vapour then travels up the "swan neck" of the still and is passed through a condenser mechanism. The condenser quickly cools the vapour causing(you guessed it) condensation. The newly condensed liquid now travels into a machine that tests for alcohol percentage. The first portion of the distillate comes in around 20% alcohol. It's called the the "low wines" this portion is sent to a container called the spirit safe. There the distiller and the on site customs and excise inspector check for alcohol percentage, and other possible problems with the low wines.

The low wines are then pumped to a second pot still for a second distillation. The same process is repeated, but now the distiller must begin to test the output of the condenser. The first portion of liquid released from the condenser is known as the fore shots, this is essentially stinky poison. But the stinky poison is redirected back into the second still for a kind of half distillation. About 45 minutes into the process the fore shots end and you get the "spirit" this comes out of the condenser usually crystal clear and very neutral in smell and flavour. This run usually lasts a couple hours and it's the stuff that us going to make your scotch. It comes in between 65-75% alcohol and it's again tested and catalogued by the distiller and the customs man. Every ounce of alcohol in this process is accounted for by the distiller and audited on site by a government official.

As the spirit run ends another run called "the feints" is produced. This is again separated, catalogued and redistilled. The feints can be very interesting, full of flavour packed oils and quite aromatic so they add character to the spirit. They can also be quite toxic so this must be controlled.

Maturation:

So when you have your spirit you essentially have very very labour intensive scottish vodka. Anything that comes out of a still is known as a neutral spirit. There is very little flavour or character. This is where maturation comes into play. Whisky gets it colour and much of it's flavour from the wood it is aged in. The spirit is placed in barrels which have been charred in the inside. There barrel are not brand new as well. They have in the past carried usually American Bourbon or Spanish Sherry.**** These barrels can cost upwards of $3000 USD, and normal aging house can have thousands of barrels and millions of dollars of equipment to move, store and catalogue.

During the maturation process the volume of alcohol in the barrel that is lost to evaporation is normally 2% a year, this is called the angels share. 100 litres of spirit over ten years of evaporation would be about 82 litres. Those angels love to drink. You can image the expense which a distillery incurs when you're losing that much product just to the air.

As I explained in my Introduction to Scotch, the age statements and marring process are a science all their selves and I am at over 1500 words so I figure this may be a great place to leave off.*****

After seeing the process and cost that goes into the production of single malt you can begin to see why it is so expensive. If you got to this point I admire the commitment.

*The Scots are like Natives in that nothing in the process goes to waste. 2nd and 3rd washes are usually reused in subsequent batches. The second wash becomes the first wash in the next batch, the third wash becomes the second and so on. Also these "washes" can be used in the production of beer or barley wine.

**Yeast is a single celled organism that in the case of fermentation eats sugars and craps out alcohol and carbon dioxide. Yeast makes bread rise because it eats sugar and releases carbon dioxide that carbon dioxide creates pockets in the dough thus the rising effect.

***It's also important to note that during this phase there must be an absolute sterile environment. The environment for yeast to propagate is also the perfect environment for bacteria. A bacterial taint can ruin a whole batch of wirt.

**** Whisky can be aged in lots of different types of barrels from Port to Tokaji. What resided in the barrel before the spirit goes in can affect the flavour and colour of your whisky in dramatic ways.

*****Ok so as promised I am going to tie this up by telling you how dumb it is to spend over 30 dollars on a bottle of vodka. The process of making vodka isn't unlike the process of making scotch in that grain is converted to sugar and then girst, then wirt, then beer, then spirit. But when vodka is produced the producer buys the cheapest grist they can buy, they use a continuous still that allows you to just feed beer in one end and after three distillations the vodka comes out of the final condenser, it's diluted to 40%, filtered and bottled. The cost on a bottle of vodka is about a dollar. 95 cents for the bottle and 5 cents for the liquid. So find a lower priced vodka you like and drink it while you laugh at the chuckle heads who are drinking a 50 dollar bottle of the exact same product.

Drinks You Should Know: The Hot Toddy

I love my friend's kids, they are well behaved, thoughtful, entertaining little bundles of joy. But because I am childless man I have yet to be exposed the gauntlet of germs by which a parent's immune system is tempered. So after a great weekend of visiting friends with all of my friends with kids my throat began to get scratchy and my nose filled. By this morning I have downgraded my condition from a scratchy throat and the sniffles to a raw throat and a chest cold.*

However, there is a way to make a cold more manageable and fun, the hot toddy. Thought to have been invented in Wales or Scotland the hot toddy paired scotch whiskey, with hot water or hot milk, lemon and honey to create a phlegm busting, throat soothing, sleep inducing drink that would put you and your cold under the table.

How the hot toddy works is pretty simple. Warm liquid soothes a raw or congested throat. The acidity of the lemon breaks down phlegm as well as a nice hit of Vitamin C. The honey soothes the throat, contains enzymes that break down mucous and promotes melatonin production and thus a deeper sleep. The alcohol is a central nervous system depressant which helps with cough suppression, sleep and a general feeling of awesome.

Of course there now are regional takes on the hot toddy which work for all different climates, regional spirits and ingredients.

In the American South a hot toddy is made with Bourbon, tea, citrus fruits and cinnamon.

In the American Southwest and Mexico, tequila, citrus juice, cinnamon and other spices.

In Japan there is a cold remedy called Tamagozake which is a mixture of Warm Sake, sugar and a raw egg.**

In India, Chai tea is mixed with scotch whisky and various spices as a cold remedy.

If you are actually sick there is nothing better than sleep, fluids and chicken soup but if you are actually sick please see a doctor instead of drinking some kind of crazy Japanese sake-nog.

---

*Though I am free from tummy aches, the poops, pinkeye, and ebola virus.

**You drop a nuclear weapon on a culture and this is what you get. I love you Japan but sometimes you be crazy.

Foods You Should Know: A Drunken Love Letter To Shawarma

I am going to let everyone in on a secret about this blog. I write everything in advance and then I let it marinate for up to a few weeks, I then edit(sometimes poorly) and then I post. This post was written at about 3 am after drinking way too much and having MacDonald's after the bar. Obviously I was lusting for something better and I really didn't get where I was going, but I feel as if you read this after a night at the bar you would agree. I decided to not do more than a quick edit because I wanted to show off what a totally inebriated unfocused mind has to say about what it craving in the moment. To the people of Israel, the heavily eyebrowed and the over sensitive please accept my deepest apologies.

Shawarma is the reigning king of street food and if you're from Windsor you should know what it's all about.

Shawarma, Donair, Kebab, Gyros no matter what you call it it's the best possible decision you can make when it's two AM on a Friday night. Pizza is passé, hot dogs are for five year olds, but shawarma is what grown ups eat when they are getting drunk like teenagers.

So what is shawarma? Where does it come from? And most importantly why do I crave the shit out of it after a night of abusing my liver?

The word Shawarma comes from the Arabic for turning, which describes the large pieces of lamb, chicken, beef, or sometime goat that is spit roasted. The meat is sliced off the turning spit and put on a pita with lettuce, tomatoes and all kinds of other pickled vegetables, hummus, garlic sauce and tahini (sesame seed paste). The pita is then wrapped up and pressed in a sandwich press to make a conical home for all of the great stuff inside.

Shawarma comes from the Middle East. I have heard Lebanese, Egyptian, Greek, and Turk all lay claim to being the creators and masters of the rotating meat, but it's more of a ubiquitous street food found all over the world. In the Middle East I would venture a guess that much of the regional strife is caused by a deep seeded zeal about who produces the best shawarma. That and Israel, and maybe oil but mostly who makes the best shawarma.

So why does shawarma comfort me when my liver is giving me the cold shoulder? I think that is the question that escapes us all. It's warm, it's filling, it's full of sweet, salty and spicy. It is made right in front of you by a man who's expression is held squarely in his anabolic eyebrows, who is somewhere between indifferent and asleep. The din of Middle Eastern music and discussion wakes up your whiskey soaked mind, so that you can haggle cab far like you are in a bazaar in Riyadh*

The other part of a 2 am shawarma visit is the side dishes. Can you get roasted potatoes with garlic sauce at pizza pizza? You get a dipping sauce for your subpar pizza and a can of Pepsi. Can you get rice with lentils or tabbouleh at a street meat cart? If you answer is yes, please point me to said cart. Can you get baklava at 2am anywhere else? I guess the answer is should you get baklava at 2 am?**

*Jesus, I am sorry for that paragraph. I am keeping it in because it may be the most authentically dumb thing I've written in this book and my readers deserve it.

** The answer is, of course you should.

Now this recipe is probably going to disappoint at least part of the population of the people who try it. As you may or may not have read in my article about Pho, I place a lot of stock in the broth*. I am going to try and speed up the process of making a great rich broth. And I am going to keep the rest of the process pretty simple.

The Broth:

Ingredients: 1 Oxtail

4 Marrow bones**

2 1 lb. pieces Beef chuck

2 large Onions (chopped)

1 oz of Ginger root (grated)

1/4 Cup of Fish sauce

2 tbs Sugar

2 Star Anise (whole)

5 Cloves (whole)

1 Cinnamon (stick)

1 tbs Sea salt

Directions: In a large stock pot on medium/high in grape seed oil. Brown the oxtail, marrow bones, and the pieces of beef chuck. This process should take 15 to 20 minutes of really doing well to sear all of the flavouring components. Remove all the sear beef parts and reserve them. Add the two onions and sweat them. Then add grate the ginger root, sugar, star anise, cloves, cinnamon, and sea salt. Allow the onions and ginger to begin to char. Then deglaze the pot with fish sauce and bring to a boil. Then add six litres of water and bring to boil. Once boiling, return your meat and bones to the soup, bring the heat down to simmer, cover and wait for about 2 hours. Prepare another pot with a sieve above it. Before you pour remove the bones and meat as they are large and may make a mess if they are poured. Pour the remaining contents of the stock pot slowly out through the sieve. You want to separate all the solids out of the stock. Once done you begin the soup.

*This is a wonderful soup broth pun for all of you readers who just love puns about broth.

**Bones carry so much flavour, nutrients and also gelatin. For a soup a good amount of gelatin from bones can really add tons of richness and thickness to a broth. Between the Oxtail and the marrow bones there is more than enough big flavours and gelatin going into this broth.

*** If you just slightly freeze a raw cut of beef like sirloin you are able to cut much thinner slices off it with your well sharpened knife.

****What I love about Pho is that you can use all the different ingredients to customize your soup.

The Soup:

Ingredients

5 L Homemade broth

1 large cut Sirloin (slightly frozen)***

20 Crimini mushrooms (quartered)

Rice noodles (medium thickness)

Cilantro

Mint leaves

2 cups Bean sprouts

4 Limes (quartered)

Thai bird chilies (thinly sliced)

Sriracha sauce

Hoisin sauce

Directions:

In the stock pot bring the broth to a simmer. In another pot bring water to a boil and add your noodles, this should take about 10 minutes. Once the noodles are done put them in the bowl along with your sliced raw beef, and mushrooms(and whatever other things you like in your Pho). Pour the hot broth into the bowl. This will flash cook the contents of your bowl. Enjoy!****

Foods You Should Know: Pho

Comfort food comes in many forms, but when it comes to comforting soups who would have thought that a tropical country would create the best one.

Pho* is a Vietnamese noodle soup which is a Vietnamese street food that came about in the 1920s. It has many different derivations based upon regionality but generally it is a beef noodle soup with a mix of vegetables, different cuts of meat and garnishes**.

Vietnam became a French colony in the 1860's as part of the larger colony of French Indonesia. During this time some French traditions intermingled with traditional Vietnamese and Han Chinese fare. The Oxford English Dictionary actually credits the French term Pot-au-feu as the root of the word Pho. Pot-au-fau is a classic French peasant dish of stewed beef offal***, and vegetables which really does resemble Pho.

In my opinion the key to great Pho is the broth. Generally the broth takes all day to cook as it consists of marrow bones, oxtail, flank steak, caramelized onions and other veggies, and variety of spices ranging from star anise to cardamom. I find way too often pho places use weak broth and no matter how good the rest of the ingredients are if the broth isn't good it's all over.

What is great about pho is that so many different things can go into it. I am a huge fan of rare beef pho, which almost thin raw strips of beef are dropped into hot soup table side and are cooked by the ambient heat of the soup in the bowl. Also pho with tripe and tendon can be very tasty as the flavour of the not so caught after meat does wonders in mixing with the flavour of the broth. I've also had seafood versions with fish meat balls, squid and shrimp. There are dozens of different kinds of Pho and it's a great way to expand your food horizons in a very familiar comforting way.

The garnishes are also very important to pho. The flavour, textures and aroma of the soup is a very personal thing. I love a spicy version of the soup with lots of chili sauce, some Thai basil and a little bit of hoisin sauce for a sweet tang. Some people love to squeeze limes into the soup to give it a more sour base of flavour. It's a very cool way to allow the eater to tailor the dish to his or her own likes and dislikes.

Overall if you have never had pho, go out this week and try it. It may be sweltering hot out but hot soup actually makes you swear which will cool you down. Enjoy!

*The pronunciation of the word Pho is one of those hotly debated things that I could give a quarter of a fuck about. I always pronounced it "FOE" while I have heard derivations of "fuh", "fah" and the most pitied of them all "Foo".

**Thai Basil, Lime, bean sprouts, fish sauce, hoisin sauce, chili sauce, etc

***Offal is a term for those parts of the animal that most people don't want to eat. Tongue, tail, feet, brains, tripe, lung, etc

Braised Chicken Thighs in A Spicy Ragu.

I noticed while looking though the recipes I've published that there is only one chicken recipe. One of the most underused, delicious and inexpensive cuts of the chicken is the thighs. The meat is moist and flavourful, the skin is leaner than most of the rest of the chicken and the bones carry tonnes of flavour. This recipe is a take on the classic chicken cacciatore but with more of a rustic feeling to the ragu.

Ingredients:

4 Chicken thighs (bone in, skin on)*

1 large Red onion (rough chopped)

2 cloves Garlic (diced)

2lLarge Carrots (1/2 in chop)

2 stocks of Celery (finely chopped)

1 fennel bulb (rough chopped)**

1 large can of diced tomatoes (in their juice)

1 cup Dry white wine

Chicken stock

1 tube Polenta (cut into 1/4 inch thick discs)

Sea salt

Black pepper

Paprika

Chili flakes

Cayenne pepper

Olive oil

*You can totally do boneless but it does effect how flavourful the dish is. This is a pretty light dish so a little extra fat to add some richness won't kill you.

**Fennel has four components that all can add that anise flavour to a dish in different quantities. The bulb is very mild in flavour, the frawns are a little bit more flavourful, the seeds are even more flavourful and the pollen is amazingly pungent.

Directions: Set your oven at 350. In a dutch oven on medium heat add olive oil. Take your chicken thighs and coat them in sea salt, pepper, and paprika. Add your chicken thighs and sear them until the chicken skin is crisp. Remove the chicken and place on a paper towel. Add your onions and garlic and sweat. Then add your carrots, celery, fennel bulb, chili flakes and cayenne pepper and increase the heat to medium/high. Sauté the mixture until the veggies begin to intensify in colour. Then deglaze with the wine. Allow the wine to reduce by half and add the tomato. Bring heat down to a simmer and return the chicken thighs to the dutch oven. Add the chicken stock, cover, put the dutch oven into your preheated over, and set the timer for 40 minutes.

In a deep sauce pan add a generous amount of grape seed oil and bring heat to medium/high. Take the polenta disks and fry them in the oil until they begin to turn golden brown and are hard when touched. Remove the polenta, towel off the excess oil and add salt and pepper.

When plating make a bed of polenta, and spoon the chicken thighs and ragu on top. Find some of that fennel frond that is sitting on your counter, garnish and enjoy.

Recipe Redux

With the richness of chicken thigh and the spice and acidity of the sauce a wine with some softness and spice I find really would work well with this dish. As much as Sideways derided Merlot I love the varietal when done well. Chateau St. Jean Sonoma Merlot is a great example of what Merlot can do. Soft and powdery in it's mouth feel, but with bold blueberry and plum notes make this the perfect pairing with the acidity of the sauce and the richness of the meat.   Usually I am all about weird or out of the box pairings but this one is sort of a classic. Give it a try.

I don't normally centre out products on this blog but it's christmas and what is more appropriate for the celebration of the birth of a jewish kid in a barn than me telling you what kind of scotch you should buy for your boss to impress him.

Scotch over Wine:

Whenever someone asks me what kind of wine they should buy their husband/boss/brother/ barber. I always say, get them a bottle of scotch instead.   Why is scotch a better present than wine?

You need to really know the person you are buying for when it comes to wine. People are particular about what they like when it comes to wine.   If you are not clear on what the person you are buying for likes in a wine, you may be buying something they totally hate. The same is true for scotch, there are always ones people dislike, but unlike wine scotch is something you don't need to drink the entire bottle of once it is opened. Scotch can be hidden away and given ounce by ounce to guests who may enjoy that style. If you are going to spend $50 on a gift choose scotch it's a safer bet.

Scotch is something that if you collect it*, after a few years through some personal purchases and maybe a gift or two you have a range of stuff that will please anyone who comes over. It's a great thing to have a range of different scotches, something for before dinner, something for after dinner, something you want to pour a glass of after shoveling the driveway**.   Also there are different social grades of scotches. Brother in Law scotch is just as valuable to a collection as the scotch you serve to the person who bought you your first good bottle. You want something in your collection that you can serve to the guy in a mock turtle neck who is the husband of one of your wife's friends, without wasting your 1966 Tullibardine.

What To Buy This Christmas:

Under $50

Te Bheag, $36: Blended whisky either gets not nearly enough credit or way too much credit depending on who you come across. Te Bheag*** is one of the most well made blended scotch whiskies on the market and for it's rock bottom price point it will blow your mind. Produced on the Isle of Skye this whiskey is rich, sweet and just a little bit peaty.

Under $75

Auchentoshan 12, $52: Auchentoshan is known by many scotch drinkers as breakfast whisky. A triple distilled single malt delivers a very light bodied spirit packed with lots of big flavours of dried fruit and spice. With super cool modern packaging this whiskey looks as great as it tastes. It will not fail to impress the beginner or the veteran alike. And the price is great.

AnCnoc 12, $65: AnCnoc is a product from the Knockdhu distillery in the highlands near Inverness. With notes of citrus and vanilla this pale coloured whiskey delivers tons of bang for the buck. The mouthfeel is heavy on this one but it also has some great liveliness left in it. I am a huge fan of this one.

Under $100:

Bowmore Tempest 10, $77: Bowmore is one of my favourite Islay whiskies because of its interplay between smokey peat and beautiful chocolate and citrus notes. The Tempest 10 takes all of those things and offers it in a cask strength offering. Coming in at over 55% alcohol this scotch will deliver but I would recommend putting a little distilled water in just to smooth it out.

Glenfarclas 105, $90: Glenfarclas is one of my all time favourites and this offering is one of the best values in all of scotch. The 105 is a cask strength whisky that comes in at 60% alcohol. It needs to be diluted because it will make you mouth go numb but when you find the right level of dilution it is an explosion of flavour. From caramel apple to sour cherry to almost a cigar box smokiness. This whisky is one of the most complex I've ever tasted.

Under $200

Highland Park 18, $150: This whisky is all about balance. Highland Park gives you a little bit of everything. Sweetness, spice, smokey peat and elegant mouthfeel. Aged in sherry casks this whiskey from the Isle of Orkney is one of the best examples of an 18 year old whisky actually being worth its price tag.

Bunnahabhain 18, $160: This Islay malt isn't over the top with peat but instead plays a beautiful game of balancing a sweet creme brûlée front end with a smoky and earthy peat back end. If you are unsure about your first foray into a peaty whisky this is a winner. It will give you an idea of what Islay can do but with a rewarding, warm sweet front palate.

Price is No Object

Gordon and McPhail 1958 Glen Grant, $650: Gordon and McPhail are one of the most renown independent bottlers of all time and their 1958 vintage of Glen Grant is a mind blower. Toffee and Christmas spice are the big notes on this gem, but they fade into mellow pear and malt flavours. I had this one at a tasting in Calgary, traded jackets with my boss and went up again to get another sample. It's a stunner and at $650 a bottle it's actually kind of a deal.

The Skyline, Masters of Photography, The Macallan, $????: This super limited edition of The Macallan features famed photographer Annie Lebowitz shooting scottish actor Kevin McKidd in different settings. This 1996 vintage scotch is 15 years old and included a limited edition Annie Lebowitz print. Previous Masters Of Photography series bottles went for upwards of $5,000.

Overall you can get great value in scotch at any price point. It's all about having a balanced collection so that in a pinch you're not pouring the good stuff for someone who doesn't deserve it.

*And you don't just plow through every bottle in your possession compulsively.

**i.e Something peaty and warming.

***Pronounced "Che Veck" not "Tea Bag".

Foods You Should Know: Montreal Smoked Meat

"You know if you had really, really been intent on entrapping me on my wedding night, you wicked woman, you would not have dabbed yourself with Joy, but in Essence of Smoked Meat. A maddening aphrodisiac, made from spices available in Schwartz's delicatessen. I'd call it Nectar of Judea and copyright the name."-Mordecai Richler

Montreal is a great food city. It is a blend of Parisian flair and a rustic New World sensibility, which makes it a lively and surprising culinary experience. The one thing that defines Montreal's food identity is not classic French cuisine. It's a sandwich that couldn't be any less French.

Montreal Smoked Meat defines Canadian deli, in the same way as pastrami defines New York deli. Jewish Immigrants from all over Eastern Europe flooded Montreal at the turn of the century. They brought kosher butchering and charcuterie methods that had been refined and influenced in Europe for hundreds of years.

Montreal Smoked Meat is a beef brisket which has been dry cured in salt, black peppercorns, coriander, and a variety of other spices. This curing process last ten days and then the meat is hot smoked and then steamed before serving. * There are usually four different cuts of meat. Lean, medium, medium-fat and fat. They all come from the same cut of meat but from different locations in the brisket.

The Montreal smoked meat sandwich is a simple but subtle art**. It may look like deli anarchy, but there is a lot that goes into making a great sandwich. First the bread, it needs to be rye and it needs to be seedless. Second the meat, hand cut across the grain usually about a centimetre thick. I like a grainy mustard with the sandwich as it adds some textural elements to the ultra tender meat. The bread can be pressed and toasted a bit, but if the bread is fresh I don't see the point. The sides are usually a kosher dill pickle, some coleslaw with a simple vinaigrette and some chips for a crunch. A perfect lunch.

Now that you know what goes into a smoked meat sandwich I am going to blow your mind. At a breakfast joint in Guelph, someone with a much higher IQ than myself figured out that if you take Montreal smoked meat, throw it on a griddle and serve it as a breakfast side instead of bacon or ham, people will come. Angel's Diner changed my outlook on smoked meat.

You mean you can use deli meat in something other than a sandwich? Yes you can. I have had Smoked meat poutine, wonderful! I've made Smoked meat omelettes, smoked meat fritatas, and my personal favourite. Beef Rouladen stuffed with smoked meat, Swiss cheese, mustard and sauerkraut.

What is funny to me is that of the many smoked briskets I've made/eaten Montreal Smoked Meat is not really all that smokey. I know that the name refers to the process more than the flavour but to those who've never had real smoked brisket, it's kind of a surprise. Also pastrami(New York's answer to smoked meat) has an ungodly amount of sugar used in its curing process, smoked meat has almost none.

**A dish that is simple does not mean easy. Simple means that there is nowhere for a screwup to go hide. If the meat is cut too thin you make a mess, if there is too much mustard you kill the flavours of the meat. If the bread is not fresh you might as well pack it in and open a pharmacy.*

WINTER:

"Au milieu de l'hiver, j'apprenais enfin
qu'il y avait en moi un été invincible."
-Albert Camus

I want my winter food to be an uplifting reprieve from the cold unless you are doing it really right and cooking on your barbecue regardless of the temperature.

For me winter is a difficult season. The lack of sunlight affects my brain in ways that make it difficult for me to function at my best. Anxieties increase, depression creeps in and sometimes when you are in those states a good comforting meal is the best remedy. I have always found the act of cooking therapeutic something relaxing that allows me to turn my brain off and something that also gives an immediate sense of accomplishment. You know when you've cooked something properly there is little room for neurosis. Not to mention, that it's great to cook for others, being of service to friends and family is a great way to step outside of your own head.

Winter is time also to be warmed by rich red wine and even richer smokier scotches. Nothing beats coming in from shoveling the driveway and enjoying a dram of Ardbeg or a glass of Cabernet Franc from Maremma.

My winter food is about celebration, it's about getting together with friends and family and maybe going a little bit over the top with the richness.

Living for Calgary for five years I learned that my winters growing up in Southern Ontario were nothing to complain about, those long cold winters did teach me how to really create a hearty meal. Bacon and Potato Leek soup, Kim Chi Stew, and Quick Roast Chicken are all dishes in this chapter which will show you how to warm and comfort while also elevating food to a different level.

My winter food is really about integrating aggressively spiced foods with comforting flavours and textures. Spicing doesn't mean heat necessarily. Clove and cinnamon are two of my favourite winter accents for savory food.

Though winter is my least favourite time of year, the food I make in Winter is some of my most favourite share this food with your friends and family from me and mine.

Pub food is something that I love on a rainy day. It's rich, warming and it always works well with a pint in your hand. I am always a fan of steak and Guinness pie and this is my twist on that. I am not much of a baker and my skills with pastry hover somewhere between shitty and disastrous. So assume that you're better at me at using Robin Hood pre made pie crust mix. The filling is really what matters.

Ingredients: I have no business telling you how to do a pie crust. I use Robin Rood mix in a Pyrex pie plate with a lattice top to the pie. But do whatever you want.

2.5 lbs of Beef cheek (this is usually 2 cheeks)*

1 Onion (rough chopped)

2 Cloves of Garlic (rough chopped)

2 Yukon gold potatoes (1/2 inch dice)

2 Carrots (cut thick)

2 Purple turnips (1/2 inch dice)

1 Star anise

1/2 tsp Cumin seed

1 tsp Turmeric

1 tsp Coriander

1 tsp Dried mustard seed

1 tsp Cracked black pepper

1 bottle English brown ale**

1.5 cups Beef stock

1 tbs Maple syrup

1 Thai chili (whole)

*If you've never had beef cheek before, it's a fantastic and cheap cut. But here are the draw backs. It needs to be braised for a few hours, and you usually have to preorder it from your butcher. Brisket can work for this dish but the texture of the cheek works so much better.

**I like using Newcastle for this. It's easy too find, and bang on flavour wise for what you need.

Directions: Make your pie crust and lattice and don't ask me how to do it because you will be disappointed in my fear of pastry. In a dutch oven with oil, sear your beef cheeks at a high temp. You want to get a nice crust on the meat as the cut is quite lean and you can't afford to lose the juices it does have. Then reduce heat to medium and add your onions and garlic, until they sweat. Deglaze with the beer. Add your potatoes, carrots, and turnips. Really let those veggies cook down for about 10 minutes stirring regularly and deglazing just a little with beer if necessary. Then add your spices, the chill pepper, the rest of the beer and enough beef stock to cover your meat and veggies. Put the dutch over in an oven at 350 for 90 minutes. Remove the dutch oven from the oven and make sure the beef is fork tender. If its not, add a little more stock and cook for another 30 minutes. When the beef is fork tender remove it onto a cutting board and let it rest. Take the dutch oven and put it back on medium heat. You are going to want to reduce the mixture in the pot until it's a thick gravy consistency. You then shred the beef into a pulled pork kind of consistency. Begin to add the beef to the pie shell and then ladle the veggie and curry gravy mixture to the pie shell place the lattice on top of the contents and then pour the maple syrup onto the top of the lattice. Put back into the over for 30 minutes. The maple syrup should crisp up the lattice and ooze into the filling, the sweetness should work well with the big aromatics and spice in the filling. When the top of the pie is golden brown remove from the oven and let it rest for 10 minutes. Then cut and serve with a bottle of that beer.

This is a spicy dish so I really do advocate drinking a beer with it and do your best to fish the star anise out of the gravy as it can be unpleasant to accidentally bite into. Enjoy!

Recipe Redux
Newcastle Brown Ale is a classic that will work amazingly with this dish for two reasons. First it's used in the cooking of the dish and second it's a beautifully rich flavoured but light palleted beer that will cool the mouth while complimenting the pie. If you want to play a little differently Granville Island Lions Winter Ale would work beautifully as well. With notes of earl grey tea and a rich malty backbone it will compliment and contrast the rich spicy meat pie.

Foods You Should Know: Kim Chi

Korean cuisine is something I feel more people should try*. It is the most rustic of the Asian cuisines. Grilled meats, hearty seafood soups and stews, strange but fantastic savory pancakes and a condiment that goes into everything.

Kimchi or Gimchi or Kimchee or Kim Chi depending how you want to spell it is more than just a staple of Korean cuisine, it's a national obsession. There are literally dozens of different varieties of this most times hot, sometimes briny, fermented, Napa cabbage based condiment.

Kimchi is usually made out of Napa Cabbage, green onions, radish, ginger, garlic, red chillies, and some kind of briny or fishy base. Kimchi in Korea is very region. Some areas like their kimchi less spicy and more salty, some use anchovy sauce or fish sauce as a base, kimchi from some areas will make the back of your eyes burn. It all depends on the regional cuisine and what kind of flavour profile the kimchi needs to compliment.

Kimchi also has seasonal styles. As the cabbage is harvested once and Kimchi is a fermented dish throughout the year the flavour and style will change because of the different lengths of fermentation. Also different seasonal veggies are used to accent the kimchi. Spring kimchi has little to no real fermentation and shades more towards an herbal flavour. Summer has cucumber and radish and a little stronger flavour, fall kimchi moves towards salty and briny flavours as the weather cools. And winter kimchi is the heartiest. It usually has a variety of nuts, more heat and a very strong fermented flavour, essentially trying to pack as much energy into the condiment as possible.

So what is kimchi like to a western palate? The best way I can describe its texture is a chunky and more watery version of coleslaw which has a very deep and rich flavour to it. The heat can range from fiery to subtle but it's not cheap** front of the palate heat it's more something that comes on fifteen seconds after you chew and swallow.

Kimchi also is touted for its health benefits. It's very high fibre, and low calorie. It contains garlic, and ginger which have natural antiseptic qualities and have been proven to decrease inflammation and boost the immune system. The lactic acid produced in the fermentation process aids digestion, and has anti-cancer links. Spicy food actually helps battle depression and chronic pain as specific parts of the brain is stimulated by the pain and heat reaction of the capsaisin in the peppers.

I didn't want to do an over arching piece on all Korean cuisine because I felt like it may end up like my Sushi articles which was much too long. So I felt as if talking about Kimchi would explain to someone who may one day try Korean food would get at least the logical through line that is Kimchi.

*Sometimes I like to make my reader squirm with these pieces. Korean cuisine is the most accessible of the Asian cuisines in my opinion, as long as you can handle some heat.

** Cheap heat is something I may have made up or I may have stolen from someone, I truly can't remember. I describe it as that flavour you get when someone just tosses Cayenne Pepper into or onto a dish to give it heat without actually developing its flavour. Cheap heat hits you right on the tip of your tongue and burns your palate out. Good heat comes on slower, it burns in the back and sides of your tongue and mouth and it can be painful hot but it never really impedes flavour. It comes with developing your flavour and heat over time and not just tossing hot stuff in at the end in a cheap attempt to achieve heat.

Korean cuisine doesn't really get its due as one of the most approachable and flavourful of all Asian cuisine. Here is a great way to warm up after a cold fall day. It's hearty and spicy but also comforting, which kind of explains its production and different regional tweaks. For this recipe we will be using bottled Kim Chi which I am sure would get my ass kicked by a Tae Kwon Do champion but this is how it has to be since I don't expect people to ferment their own cabbage and chilies. This recipe is a take on a classic Korean dish called Kimchichigae but I give it a few of my own touches.

Ingredients:

200 g Smoked bacon (cut into very small pieces)

1 lb. Short ribs (deboned)

Short rib bones*

Sesame seed oil

3 cups Beef stock

2 Cups Kim chi (choose your brand)

1 Onion (diced)

3 cloves Garlic (rough chopped)

1 tbs Sriracha chili sauce

1 tbs Crushed red chilies

1 tbs Fish sauce

1 large Daikon** (cubed)

*The bones are super important to adding thickness and flavour to this broth.

**A large phallic Asian radish

Directions:

In an oiled dutch oven on medium heat add onions and sweat until translucent. Pre heat your oven to 325. Then add bacon and render the fat off the bacon and add the garlic again cooking down the garlic. Take your short rib meat and cover it in the Sriracha sauce and crushed red chili flakes. Turn up heat in the dutch oven to medium/high and sear the rib meat. Add your rib bones and continue to stir. Then add your Daikon to the dutch oven and keep stirring. If you need to deglaze just used a little bit of the beef stock just to make sure nothing burns. Then add your fish sauce and Kim Chi and reduce by half while you continue to stir the contents. The contents of the dutch oven should be a deep red with brownish hues to it. After about 15 minutes of stirring the mixture and reducing. Add your beef stock bring to a boil and remove from heat. Cover the dutch oven and place in the preheated oven. Let the contents cook for about 2.5 hours, remove from oven, fish out the rib bones and serve.

The stew should be thinner than most stews you are used to because of the acidity of the Kim Chi and chili sauce. The daikon should be very tender and exploding with flavour and the meat should melt in your mouth. Step out of the box this fall and try a Korean take on comfort food.

Recipe Redux

Again I will pair a beer with a soup or stew for many reasons but mostly because hot soup and wine do not match well together. With this dish I choose Korean rice beer Hite. This super light easy drinking lager will remind you of a slightly more complex Budweiser. It will do wonders in cooling the mouth down and just kind of cleansing the pallet, just keep in mind it's bad manners not to sweat while eating Korean cuisine.

This is a very basic recipe for a soup that will absolutely work as a comfort food or as something that will impress at a dinner party with only a few tweaks.

Ingredients: 6-strips Smoked bacon (cut into small pieces)

4 large Yukon gold potatoes (sliced and un-peeled)

1 large Yellow onion (rough cut)

2 Leeks (chopped fine)

2 cloves Garlic (manually crushed)

250ml Unsalted butter

2 Cups Chicken stock

2tbs Sour cream

Canola oil (as needed)

Creme fraiche (optional)

Scallions (optional)

Directions: To start, render your bacon and a medium/high heat in the same pot as the soup, make sure that you are getting some nice crispness.* Drop your heat to medium and add onions and sweat them in the bacon fat add small amounts of Canola oil as needed if there isn't enough bacon fat. Add leeks and garlic and let all of those ingredients marry with the onions and bacon. Add Potatoes.* The longer that you can keep all of these components in the pot without burning or having them stick to the bottom of the pot, the more you are going to integrate all the the flavours into the potatoes. You then add your butter and sour cream let that melt in and then add your stock. Stir, Cover, Simmer. This all should simmer for about 45 minutes. I personally like to let soups go for longer (2 hours)than that because I find that the flavours deepen and change over that extra time. After the simmering time, remove your soup from the heat and give it a few minutes, grab your immersion blender and you are going to be turning into a silky texture.** Make sure that you are putting your blender just above the surface every so often so that you can inject a little air into the soup. After your soup is in a bowl a great way you bring this soup up another notch is to add a dollop of creme fraiche some roughly chopped scallions and a sprinkle of some of that bacon you saved from the beginning of the cooking process.

*Remove 1/3 of the bacon preferably the crispier pieces from the pot and wrap in paper towel

**Un-peeled potatoes will add some great texture to the soup. Because we will be immersion blending this soup we need textural components like the crispy bacon we have saved in the paper towel and the potato skin to make sure our soup doesn't remind us of baby food.

***Make sure when you are using an immersion blender to take the liquid off heat. I have learned this lesson the painful scarring way.

Foods You Should Know: Borscht

Eastern European cuisine gets a bad reputation for being boring or at least staunchly utilitarian. But there are some classic dishes that have very interesting regional evolutions, Borscht being one.

You can blame communism for the lack of perceived flare of Eastern European/Eurasian cuisine. It was believed by the Soviets that enjoying food for anything beyond sustenance was an affectation of the bourgeoisie, and thus frowned upon. Essentially seventy years of food culture was suppressed by this ethos but it also gives us almost a food time capsule.*

Borscht is a simple soup made from beetroot, cabbage, and tomato, though there are numerous regional and seasonal variations on those basic ingredients. The word borscht comes from the Slavic word for beat. It is also common for Borscht to be served hot and cold. My preference is a simple borscht with lots of cabbage, dill, and a topping of sour cream. I also some nice Rye bread is always welcome for dipping.

What is interesting about Borscht is the different derivations depending on region.

In Poland, Borscht is a seasonal food. Each season brings different ingredients. In the fall potatoes and bacon are added. At Christmas a vegetarian borscht. In spring hard boiled eggs and fermented barley are added. And in summer a cold borscht is on the menu.

In the southern former Soviet Union**, it is normal to have beef, yogurt, and potato added.

In the Ukraine, borscht is actually made from a beef or chicken base not a beet root base. The beats are usually chunky vegetables in the broth as well as mushrooms, and string beans.

In all borscht is an easy to make, healthy soup that can be made very light and very heavy depending on what you have in the fridge. Finding a good Eastern European restaurant in Windsor isn't tough so find a local place and give it a try.***

---

*In Soviet Russia, food judges you.

**Armenia, Azerbaijan, Uzbekistan

***Seriously give it a try, it's not an easy dish to make sound all sexy and good in text form. I can make pancakes seem erotic but Borscht not so much.

Foods You Should Know: Bone Marrow

Sometimes I like to gross people out with the things I like to eat. I once ate an octopus that was still moving, I have eaten all sorts of organ meat, raw seafood only scares me if it's not fresh, but my true love is Bone Marrow.

It was 2006 when I first was peer pressured into eating bone marrow by my cousin. He chided me for not scooping the gelatinous substance from the inside of my osso buco bones. And as soon as I tasted it I was hooked. Bone Marrow is not something you eat every day, it is rich and really not the most approachable thing to serve to guests.

In ancient times bone were more sought after than meat. They were light, portable, they could be used as weapons and tools. But they also were full of one of the richest substances in the mammalian body, bone marrow. Bone marrow has sky high caloric value, it's a great source of minerals and nutrients, the cholesterol in bone marrow are mostly comprised of low density lipoprotein* Humans were not the first to figure out the value of bone marrow. Predatory and scavenger birds have beaks that are designed to crush bone to get at the marrow. Some of the larger predatory birds, such as vultures, have been known to drop large bones from hundreds of feet in the air to smash them so that they can eat the calorie packed marrow.**

The best thing about bone marrow is that is tastes amazing. Even though the texture of bone marrow is ultra rich and velvety in texture the flavours bely it's consistency. There is a subtle nuttiness to the flavour of bone marrow, as well as a slight sweetness that comes out when it is salted.

I like my marrow with a sprinkle of coarse sea salt spread over toast. It's simple, it's flavourful and it costs almost nothing. All you do is go to your local butcher and ask him for marrow bones. You then stand them upright on a baking sheet with some oil, and salt and roast them at 350 for 15-25 minutes. You then break through a thin membrane of spongy bone and scoop out the marrow.***

I don't expect many of you to try this but if you are feeling adventurous it's an easy thing to make, to expend your food horizons.

*The "good" cholesterol.

**Now imagine a vulture production line ala The Flintstones where vultures just drop bones and other vultures harvest the marrow while one vulture looks at the camera and without an ounce of joy utters, "it's a living".

***After all that you can still make soup.

Recipe: The Perfect Pasta Bake

There are days when you just need something easy, delicious and comforting for dinner. This recipe is just that. It's a basic baked pasta dish but what I've done is switched out a few ingredients to make it a little bit more interesting.

*Fusilli Jerry? Let's see if more than one person gets that reference.

Recipe Redux: Pasta with meat sauce is actually a little bit trickier to pair than just opening a bottle of Chianti.   A pasta bake screams for acidity to cut the fat in the cheese and meat. Chianti can fit the bill but I would recommend trying something more interesting. Barberesco is a wine from Langhe, Piedmonte in northern Italy. Barberesco comes from the Nebbiolo grape and is quite dry and acidic. Prunotto Barberesco is my pick for this one. Another Antinori family production that balances spice, floral and gamey notes that contrast the pasta bake well, and bring the flavours of the wine to a different level.

** Pecorino Romano is a cheap and high quality alternative to Parmesano Reggiano. I actually like it better for pastas like this because you don't feel bad using a lot of it and it really gets a nice crispiness when baked.

Ingredients: 3 Cups of Fusilli*

Salt

3 Chorizo Sausages (casings off meat hand shredded)

1 tbs Olive Oil

1 Spanish Onion (diced)

3 Cloves of Garlic (diced)

1 tbs of Capers

100 g Fontina Cheese

50 g Pecorino Romano**

2 tbs Thyme (fresh, finely chopped)

2 cans of Peeled Whole Tomatoes (crush these by hand)

Directions:

In a sauce pan add olive oil heat on medium until it begins to smoke. Add Onions and garlic and sweat. Add hand shredded sausage meat and brown. Add the Thyme.   Add the tomato and juices and bring to a boil. Stir the sauce. Bring the sauce down to a simmer for 30 minutes. Add the capers and salt to taste. While the sauce is simmering bring a pot of salted water to boil. Add your fusilli and follow the directions(Usually 10-12 minutes.) Sample the pasta. You want it to be a little bit chalky still, a bit before al dente. Strain the pasta and add the cooked pasta to the sauce. Stir and make sure your pasta is totally coated in the sauce. The starch from the pasta should thicken the sauce a bit after a minute or two. Then grab a pyrex baking dish and pour the pasta and sauce in. Then layer shredded Fontina Cheese on top. Put it into a oven preheated to 375. Keep an eye on the cheese. Once it is melted remove the dish from the oven and add a layer of the Pecorino on top of the fontina. Return to the oven and wait for the cheese to get a nice golden brown crust on top. Remove from oven. Let it sit for about 10 minutes and serve.

Garnish with basil leaves and Parmigiano Reggiano.

In Vino Veritas: What I Feel And What I Know

I've spent the last four years selling and purchasing some of the most sought after and not so sought after wines in the world. I've sold on a retail level, I've purchased for a large wine boutique retailer, I've advised the purchaser of the third largest wine and spirits retailer in Canada, I've sold to retailers, I've sold to independent restauranteurs, and restaurant chains.

In those four years I learned a few things. In Vino Veritas, is going to be a series where I expound on my experience in a much different voice than you are going to see in the rest of this blog. This is going to be a bit inside, it's going to cater to wine geeks, and wine professionals. I plan on writing more accessible wine articles in the near future, but my In Vino Veritas series will not be accessible if you don't know wine.

What I feel: Wine is an art form. Winemaking is a noble, passionate endeavor. Those who make wine, be it a masterpiece or plonk, are the most down to earth, hardworking, humble people you will ever meet.

What I know: In the real world wine is a packaged good. It's a box of cereal, it's bottle of toilet bowl cleaner, it's an aisle end display if you grease the proper palms. The nobility of wine only goes as far as its ability to effect a profit and loss sheet.

What I feel: People who are studied in wine, love wine. They should want to share that passion with the rest of the world, even if it means stepping out of their comfort zone and engaging those they normally would not engage.

What I know: People who are studied in wine are elitist swine. They cling to paradigms and jargon, disguising them as tradition and structure to keep wine inaccessible. That said, a couple hours a week on Google, and a few hundred dollars to experimenting with new wines, makes you just as good a salesperson as a sommelier.**

What I feel: The public is drinking better wine, learning more about wine, and challenging the status quo upheld by those who are studied in wine. There is a new generation of people who want a deeper connection to what they drink and eat.

What I know: The public doesn't know shit and doesn't particularly care about what they drink. They want the cheapest bottle of whatever is at an aisle end or feature shelf. They don't want to make an informed decision, they want something with a cool label or a catchy name.

What I feel: The wine producers in Essex County are doing their best at growing this region. They are producing some fantastic wines, and they are embracing some tried and true business practices that have worked in Niagara and British Columbia.

What I know: The wine producers in Essex County are too traditional. They are risk adverse and they romanticize their products. This romantic attitude loses them in the shuffle before they can ever make a name for themselves. The reality is, that they don't have the capital to play ball with the rest of the Canadian wine industry so their only choice is innovation.

**This is coming from someone who has some classical wine training as well as hours of self directed learning. I would dust most sommeliers when it comes to working with the public on wine and actually selling. Yes, ISG grads that there is a challenge.

Recipe: Quick Roast Chicken w/ Grilled Root Vegetables

Before I start this recipe I am going to make a confession. I mostly stole this technique and chicken recipe from Thomas Keller. If you don't know who Thomas Keller is, Google him and go to the website for The French Laundry and do your best not to drool on your keyboard. I don't know Thomas Keller personally, but I am going to call him Tom because I feel like I've already stolen his recipe I might as well refer to him informally and disrespectfully.

The Chicken

Prep:

Preparation when working with poultry is huge and as much as vomiting for an evening or two would help my figure, I feel as though it's important not to give my readers bacterial infections. So having a clean and clear surface to work with is always a good idea. You will be handling a bird quite a bit and chicken juice is one of those things that is going to end up everywhere, it's best not to have all kinds of stuff laying around waiting to get contaminated. So the first thing you want to do is to make sure the chicken is not frozen on the inside, you do this by well for the lack of a better term fisting the carcass of the chicken.*   The next thing you should do is wash your hands. Make like Howard Hughes** and scrub those digits before you touch anything else in the kitchen. Then comes the fun part.

Ingredients: 1 full Chicken

1/2 Onion

Smoked paprika

Kosher salt

Black pepper

2 slices Bacon (julienned)

1 tbs Butter

1 full Lemon (juiced)

2 cloves Garlic (finely diced)

*Yup I just posted this blog on Facebook and all you new readers are getting chicken fisting right out of the gate. Take that gentle sensibilities.

**Yes that was a Howard Hughes reference, I like to keep things fresh and current here at Braised Blue. Join us next week when Jack Benny and I talk about what we ate the night we greased the Gerries but good.

Directions:

So my take on Tom's formula is also super simple. Inside the bird put, salt, pepper, bacon, onions, butter, lemon juice. On the outside of the bird liberally apply, salt, pepper, smoked paprika. You also do Tom's de-boning technique and trussing technique. I want to create a different flavour profile for this recipe. More of an earthy smokey chicken dish to match up with my grilled root veggies. I have found that 425 is the best temperature to cook the bird at. And usually depending on size 45 minutes should do, as long as the chicken starts off at around room temp.

The Veggies:

I love root vegetables for a bunch of reasons, natural sweetness, great and varied textures, earthy flavours, are just a few. For this dish, I love using carrots, and purple turnips.

Ingredients:

4 large Carrots (washed and unpealed)

4 medium Purple turnips (peeled and washed)

Olive oil

Balsamic vinegar

Sea salt

Pepper

Directions: Slice the carrots in half lengthwise and cut the turnips in potato chip sized slices about a centimeter thin. Toss them with the olive oil and balsamic mixture and let them sit for about 30 minutes. Then add salt and pepper. Toss them directly onto a hot grill. This should only take about four minutes per side. I like to leave a little crunch in the veggies, as well they hold onto their sweetness really well if you slightly under cook them. That sweetness will go a long way to balance the smokiness that the grill will impart on the veggies.

What is great about this is, you can really do whatever you want with the recipe flavour wise. If you want to BBQ the chicken you totally can. If you want to put a sticky rub on the chicken you can. If you want to take mercy on a poor blogger and not sue him for stealing your recipe, you can.

Foods You Should Know: Risotto

So normally when I write a "Foods You Should Know" piece I talk about the history or social inner workings of a specific food or dish. Today is going to be half recipe and half history lesson. Earlier in the week I described how to make a barley risotto. I've since been living in fear of some kind of mafia retribution for besmirching the name of risotto. Take this as a confession and penance for my food sins.*

Risotto is an Italian rice dish that is about four hundred fifty years old. Rice was brought to Italy by Arab merchants in the fourteenth century. It was considered a valuable commodity and a luxury because it was not native to Italy. That was until Italian farmers figured out that the climate in Northern and Central Italy was perfect for growing short grain rices. The production of rice exploded in Italy in the decades to come.

Like any other dish risotto grew from a varied and wide spread food culture in Italy. Risotto is generally believed to be from the Northern part of the country in the province of Lombardia. Risotto di Milanese is the most famous and basic take on risotto with only a few ingredients. Short grained rice, oil, dry white wine, onions, stock, butter and cheese. In true Italian fashion we see multiple takes on the same base dish. In Piedmonte in the northwest corner of Italy we see Risotto al Barolo, a red version of risotto, which uses the highly acidic and multifaceted wine from the Nebbiolo grape. In Veneto, in the north east of the country we see a black version of risotto that contain the ink sacks and meat of the cuttlefish.** There are so many different takes on risotto, I for instance make a mean butternut squash risotto.

When you read about risotto on the internet the word "simple" is used a lot. And that is partially true, like many Italian dishes risotto only has a few main ingredients. The trade off with simple food is that it's very easy to screw it up. If you are making a curry with twenty different ingredients it's easy to cover up a mistake, with a risotto one mistake or distraction and you will know it.

How To Make Risotto:

First and foremost you need to block off 45 minutes of your life. Once you start to make risotto there is no going back. Put your phone on silent, put on your favorite music and just got.

Ingredients: Olive oil

1 large Onion (1/4 inch dice)

1 cup Arborio rice (do not soak)

2 cups Chicken stock (heated in a pot on the stove beside your sauce pan)

1/3 cup Dry white wine.

1/2 cup Unsalted butter (room temp)

1/2 cup Parmigiano reggiano*** (grated)

Directions:

Put oil in your sauce pan, on medium/low heat. Wait for the oil to just start to smoke and add your onions. Sweat your onions until they are translucent and then add your rice. You need to be vigilant here, keep that rice moving by using a spatula or wooden spoon. Also shake your sauce pan to get an even layer of rice across the surface of the pan. You are toasting the rice, it should be about 6-8 minutes of keeping the rice moving. This is where things get interesting, you will be waiting for a smell. When the rice is sufficiently toasted you will smell almost a burnt popcorn kind of smell. When that smell comes add your white wine. The wine will be quickly soaked up by the rice and a creamy starchy substance will begin to collect in the bottom of the pan. As soon as that liquid begins to burn off add a ladle of stock. Continue to stir and reduce the stock down to that creamy white liquid, and then again add more stock. Once your stock is in you will have about twenty minutes of adding stock and reducing until your rice is tender but slightly chalky in the middle(al dente). Make sure that the risotto is a little looser(waterier) than you would normally eat it. You then add the softened butter and cheese continuing to stir. The rice will continue to cook with the ambient heat. When served the risotto should spread out on the plate if it piles up it will still taste great but true risotto needs to a little looser so that you can take some bread and soak up the creamy goodness.

Risotto is all about feel, recipes are all well and great but if you over do your rice the dish is going to suck, if you burn your rice while toasting it's going to suck, if you under do your rice, keep cooking.

So there, I feel much better about my transgressions. Hail Risotto full of starch and so on. Until next time.

*It's sunday morning, I feel as though I am cleansing my culinary soul.

**The Cuttlefish is not actually a fish. It's a cephalopod much closer to a squid or octopus.

***If you have that fake bullshit Black Diamond powdered parmesan cheese in your fridge throw it out, feel shame, and go buy a nice block of Parmigiano Reggiano and grate it as you need it.

Coffee and beef are two things to go great together and even though I am not a huge fan of beef tenderloin the flavour and texture from the espresso makes this dish really work.

The Beef

Ingredients: 2 Beef tenderloin steaks

Olive oil

Sea salt

Espresso (coarse ground)

Black pepper

Directions: Take your tenderloins and coat them in olive oil. Crust them with the sea salt, pepper, coffee. In a well conditioned cast iron skillet sear them on high heat for about four minutes on each side. This should get you to a nice rare level. You can then cook to your preferred heat. I personally prefer tenderloin very rare*, but I understand the aversion to rare meat. If you want to cook to your desired heat take the skillet after searing the steaks and oven cook them at 350 to to desired doneness. The high heat from direct cooking on the skillet is too much and can make the meat bind up a little bit, finishing in the oven will remedy this. So do whatever makes your inner fat kid happy.

* Tenderloin to me lacks texture and really loses flavour when it's cooked beyond rare. This dish really works with a great sear and a almost blue middle.

The Squash

Ingredients:

1 Butternut squash

Olive oil

Sea salt

Black pepper

Cinnamon

Gruyere (grated)

Directions: Cut the butternut squash into puck shaped pieces about 1/4 of an inch thick. Toss the pieces of squash in oil and then coat with black pepper, sea sat and cinnamon. On a heated BBQ place the squash on the grill. Cook the squash until it becomes crispy on the outside. This should take about 3-5 minutes on each side. Then add the cheese on each let melt and begin to crisp. Then remove from grill and finish with salt.

Recipe: Redux:

Beef tenderloin is not my favourite cut of beef. I find it's texture is too soft, it's flavour too muted and it's price much too high. Pairing wine with tenderloin is an even more finicky proposition. Most people just think a big California cabernet is the easiest way to go. And I agree it's a safe bet that more often than not will work nicely. But I like to really find a wine that punches up the mouth feel with some grippy tannins and big dark flavours. This is why I would go with EOS Petite Sirah with this dish. A heavy, inky black luxurious wine from Paso Robles, California. Nice dusty/grippy tannins and huge dark berry flavours will work really well with the tenderloin.

Foods You Should Know: Tourtiere

On the night before Christmas, all through the house all you could smell is the fact I can't rhyme and this fantastic Quebecois meat pie called tourtiere.*
Tourtiere is a traditional Quebecois** meat pie made around the Christmas season. Depending on where in Quebec you reside in the filling for this pie can vary. It is believe to have been created in the 1600's during the early colonization of the area by the French.

The name tourtiere comes from the traditional cooking vessel that the pie is made in, a tourte. A tourte is a medium depth, usually cast iron, basking pan. The word tourte also refers to the passenger pigeon, which was one of the common fillings for French-Canadian meat pies before their extinction. Am I blaming the extinction of passenger pigeons on the people of Quebec? Yes, your forebears were monsters.

The tourtiere that most known to Canadians is one made from finely minced pork meat, with spices such as cinnamon, clove and black pepper. This particular style of tourtiere is native to Montreal. As your travel to some of the more remote french speaking regions of Quebec you see more wild game used in tourtiere. Caribou, venison, moose, and duck are   all common as well as beef and veal(which you should never shoot for game). Not all recipes for tourtiere use only minced meat in the pie. Many times you will see potato and/or other root vegetables added into the filling usually to provide some extra moisture and texture. It's also common to use Ketchup as a condiment as the meat inside the pie can be a little bit dry. I like using maple syrup but I may get shot with a compound bow for saying that.

Without a doubt the most important part of the tourtiere is the crust. If there is thing people from Quebec do well it's protest. But if there is something else people from quebec do well, making beautiful golden brown flakey crust. Any tourtiere worth it's salt has a fuck off good crust both flakey light and rich.

Now thus far I have made it sound like tourtiere is a quebec only phenomenon but that is not true. You can pretty much find a regional variation of tourtiere all over Canada and in the North Eastern United States. On the west coast of Canada we see a smoked salmon tourtiere. In Alberta we see the use of Bison, pork and potato to give the pie a very rustic prairie feel. In the North East United States we see a more classic tourtiere but with the sweetness of maple syrup or honey added.

Now during the Christmas season you have a new mission. Find a great tourtiere recipe or one pre made from your local bakery or butcher shop. They are a crowd pleaser.

*Easily the worst thing I've written in this book. And that is the extent of my Christmasiness. Soak it all in.

**For my international readers(Yes I have international readers), Quebec is a central Canadian province which has a large French speaking population. It's cuisine is an interesting off shoot of classic French cuisine blended with the sensibility of Jewish Deli food, a love of wild game and a cold climate sensibility.

Recipe: Christmas Cornish Game Hen w/ Fois Gras Stuffing

A few years ago when I lived in Calgary my ex and I had a Christmas dinner with a few friends who were also spending the holidays away from their families. I decided to go all out on dinner and I created one of the best things I've ever made. Today, with lots of time before Christmas you get the recipe. Over the next month I will be releasing seasonal favourites.

The Cornish Game Hen is a hybrid of a Cornish Chicken and any other type of chicken and is slaughtered young (smaller than 2.5 lbs). They more or less taste like a chicken they are just miniature. What is great about them is that they take a very short amount of time to cook, they are a perfect single serving, and it's really cool to present to your guests a full bird on their plate. They also seem to have just enough room for a nice portion of stuffing*.

The Stuffing

Ingredients:

Bread crumbs (coarsely ground and oven toasted with butter, thyme and rosemary)

Shallot (fine dice)

Garlic (diced)

1/2 cup Softened butter

8 oz Fois gras (cut into 1/2 inch cubes)

1/2 cup Dried apricots (thinly slice)

Pinch of Sea salt

Black pepper (ground)

Directions: In a pan on medium heat add some olive oil and sweat your shallots. Then add garlic continue to sweat. Then add the Fois Gras and brown the livers. Then the bread crumbs, allowing them to soak up the juices from the oil and fois. The add your apricots, salt and pepper. Once all of that is cooked down add your softened butter allow that to evenly melt into the dressing. Pour the dressing into a mixing bowl, cover and place in the fridge for 2 hours. This will harden the dressing into a more manageable substance for stuffing the birds.

*Though this stuffing rocks and you'll want to make more in a casserole dish.

The Bird

Ingredients:

4 Cornish game hens

Salt water solution

Butcher's twine

Sea salt

Black pepper

Thyme

Olive oil

Butter

Pre-Made stuffing

Directions: The day before you plan to cook the hens you want to brine them in a large container full of salt water. They will spend then night taking in moisture and just enough salt to make them ultra juicy. The day of cooking remove the hens from the brine and towel dry them. Take your butter and begin to stuff the butter under then skin of the hen. This will allow the skin of the hen to really crisp but not burn. Then take your stuffing and hand stuff the bird. Then cover the bird in olive oil and rub the bird with salt, pepper, and thyme. Then truss the chicken, place the chickens on a roasting pan and put into an oven preheated to 400 degree. This should take around 45 minutes to cook but taking the internal temp of the bird is the best way to really judge the readiness(165 degrees). They should be golden brown. Let the birds sit for about 10 minutes as they will continue to cook internally then serve.

Recipe Redux:

This recipe is rich, I made it yesterday with bacon substituted with the Fois Gras and it was great. It also screamed for a good red wine with some nice acidity to give you a reprieve from all the rich. I would recommend a good Chianti Classico*. The bright acidity of the wine will work well with the richness of this dish. The tart red fruit flavours could even work as a replacement to cranberry sauce.

*When I worked for a large Albertan liquor retailer I learned that many people pronounced Chianti, She-On-Tay. The iconic Italian food wine that also sounds like a R&B singer. You'd think this is a one time thing but dozens of times I've been confronted with a person asking about a good She-On-Tay to go with their marinara sauce. So for my readers who I just embarrassed it's pronounced Key-on-Ti.

In all the recipes I've done on Braised Blue it blows my mind that I've never done mashed potatoes. I say this because it's one the the things I am really great at making. Now as you read this, you're probably thinking, "any idiot can make mashed potatoes." This is true, any idiot can make mashed potatoes but not every idiot can make them as good as I can make them. I am going to teach you a few of the tricks I've learned to make the best mashed potatoes you'll ever taste.

Ingredients:

6 large Yukon gold potatoes (soaked for 20 minutes, 1/2 thick slices)*

2 cups Salted butter

2 tbs Sour cream

1 clove Garlic

1 cup Colby cheese (finely grated)

Salt (to taste)

Black pepper (to taste)

Directions:

In a large pot filled with salted hot water place bring to a boil add your potatoes and allow them to cook until soft. This should take about 20-30 minutes depending on your water:potato ratio. Pour into a colander and allow some of the starch to drain out of the potatoes. In the same pot add half of your butter and garlic and on low heat just let the garlic sweat a little bit. Then add your drained potatoes and take off the heat. Begin to mash with a hand masher and add the rest of your butter and sour cream. Then get your immersion blender and begin to whip the potatoes slowly adding your cheese which should integrate into the potato giving it a slightly yellow tinge. Every so often with a spatula get any lumps that may be at the bottom or sides of the pot and integrate them into the blender.

After a few minutes of whipping, you should have a rich, but light and fluffy mashed potato ready to

*I love using Yukon Gold because they are not as starchy as russets or cannabecs. I find when there is too much starch in your mash potatoes they can turn out kind of gluey. This texture isn't a horrible thing but it's not a good thing either. Soaking also helps with that gluey effect. Some recipes say you soak overnight but I think that is excessive.

Foods You Should Know: Gruyere

Gruyere is the Cadillac of Swiss cheese*. It's a hard yellow cheese which hails from the town of Gruyeres which is found near Lake Geneva close to the French border.

Gruyere's production is highly regulated by the Swiss AOC system which operated much like the Italian DOC system. So here are some of the rules that come into play for the production of Gruyere. The cows that produce the milk for the cheese can only be fed grass or hay. The milk must be delivered to the cheese production facility by the dairy farmer, twice a day, and the dairy farm must be within a 20 KM radius around the production facility. The mixing vat for the cheese must be made of copper and can only be used once a day. Only the curd can be heated but not the whey. The cheese must be aged in caves with humidity no higher than 92%, between the temperatures of 12 and 18 degree celsius, while sitting on unplanned spruce shelves**. The rind of the cheese must be washed so as to visually differentiate gruyere from emmenthal. No anti microbial or colouring may be added to the rind of the cheese. The cheese can only be rubbed with water and salt. And finally only licensed cheese makers are allow to be involved with this process***.

There is a good reason for many of these seemingly harsh rules. Gruyere is made from raw milk. In North America milk must be pasteurized to kill microbes that may make people sick. Because most of the country cannot get local fresh dairy products, pasteurization is necessary. In Switzerland and most of Europe raw milk is much more common because there are more small production dairy farms which only supply locally. That and people in europe are so much tougher than North Americans, the small chance of Listeria is a gamble that is totally worth eating amazing cheeses.

Gruyere is a very versatile cheese. Younger Gruyere is great as a melting cheese, it has a mild nutty flavour and a super creamy texture. Aged Gruyere is much harder, closer to the consistency of Parmigiano Reggiano, with a more aggressive spicy flavour. Both versions are great melting cheeses for fondue or soup, but they also can be grated as a finishing cheese, and they are just great to eat on their own with some nice dry Riesling or a Bock style beer.

If you've never had Gruyere, you should start with a younger version, it's a bit more accessible and much less expensive. If you need any other cheese advice, leave a comment.

*That statement is purely based on opinion but you don't read this blog for facts do you?

**This is getting weird right?

***Ok so here is an experiment. Go buy cracker barrel cheddar cheese and then buy some cave aged gruyere. Eat them. Tell me whether or not strict government rules and control hinder the quality of a product.

Here is a simple side dish that I love because it's super easy
and rewarding. It goes with turkey, ham, lamb or pretty much any
of your classic Christmas recipes. It's great to be able to add
some heat to style of food that normally doesn't really delve
into spice. What is great about adding heat to something that is
naturally sweet is that, that balance can make something hot
much more palatable for someone who claims they don't like spicy
food.

Ingredients:

2 Butternut squash (halved and gutted)*

4 tbs Softened butter

Olive oil (as needed)

Sea salt

Pepper

D'arbola chilis (ground)

Cayenne pepper (ground)

Maple syrup

Clove

Nutmeg

*I like to half
the squash,
remove the guts
in the rounded
end, and then cut
almost a canal
down the skinny
end so that my
butter spice
mixture can get
to the entire
squash.

Directions: On a baking sheet lay your halved and prepared
butternut squash hole side up. Score the squash with a sharp
knife almost making a grid of 1/4 inch deep cuts. Rub the squash
with olive oil just enough to allow the spices to stick. Then
sprinkle on the salt, pepper, d'arbola, cayenne, clove and
nutmeg. Then top with butter and maple syrup. If the squash is
large feel free to add more butter as it really penetrates the
flesh of the squash and turns it into a creamy texture. Put in a
over preheated to 400 degrees and cook for 35 minutes. After 35
minutes remove and check the texture of the squash. Add more
butter and syrup and return to the over for another 15 minutes.
Remove from oven, wrap in foil and allow 15 minutes of sitting
time.

Service: I like to serve this dish mashed but also still on the
skin. The colours are great and presenting the thing in its skin
gives it a great look. I also like to garnish with a sprig of
fresh rosemary. Just as an aromatic not to be eaten.

Foods You Should Know: Haggis

Though I am a little bit late for Robbie Burns Day I thought it would be fun to talk about a dish that is tied to Scotland's favourite son like no other, haggis.

Known for being one of the more divisive dishes in the world haggis, is a mixture of the organ meat of a sheep(Hearts, livers and Lungs), slow simmered with minced onion, oatmeal, lard, suet, salt and a variety of spices*. All of these ingredients are traditionally placed into a sheep's stomach and simmered for between 3 and 5 hours.

Haggis itself is an interesting eating experience. Organ meat is normally quite dense but because of the long cook time and mixture of other ingredients the meat really breaks down and gets beautifully tender. While the oatmeal and suet provide a great almost nutty crunch to the dish. The spices and herbs along with the fats in the dish make for a rich, complex and very distinct culinary experience that I think everyone should at least try once in their life.

Traditionally haggis is served with neeps and tattes which is old scot for mashed potatoes and turnips.** Again an interesting play on texture and flavour with the haggis.Today many mass produced haggis no longer comes in a sheep's stomach, instead sausage casing is used because it's shelf life becomes much longer and it's mass production becomes much easier. Purists of course scoff at this, saying the sheep's stomach makes for another level of texture and flavour for the dish.

I talk about many different cuisines on this blog and I think that an open mind is the best way to try a new food. Haggis gets a bad reputation*** because it contains organ meat which already gets a bad reputation, and it is not a pretty looking dish. But if you want a truly unique culinary experience I recommend at least trying haggis. In the grand scheme of food it's really not that much different in composition to sausage.

*Black pepper, thyme, sage, parsley

**Hey Scotland, learn some English...Am I right? Just joking Scotland, once you're drunk you could be speaking Finnish and I wouldn't know the difference.

**I personally blame its depiction in the classic children's cartoon Duck Tales where Scrooge McDuck forces it on his Nephews.

The Angel's Share: Situational Drinking

There is a time and a place for a dram of single malt. Luckily there are hundreds of single malts so there in turn must me hundreds of times and hundreds of places.

Robbie Burns:

Robert Burns was born January 25th, 1759 in the village of Alloway in Scottish Highlands, near the town of Ayr. He grew up in poverty working as a manual labourer on a farm. Though not formally educated, he learned to read English, French and Latin. As a young adult Burns was a labour leader, song writer, and poet. His most famous work is the traditional Scots folk song, Auld Lang Syne.*

By 1786, Burns was published and had moved to Edinburgh to continue is writing. Burns was a proponent of writing with native Scottish language and dialect, a rejection of the anglicization of his country. For this Burns became more than just a writer in Scotland. He also took many traditional Scottish folk songs from the spoken tradition to the page. He became a symbol for Scots who had left the homeland, because of the traditionalism and inherent "Scottishness"** of his writings.

Burns also had a healthy appetite for the drink, as anyone who writes seems to. He wrote on his love of whisky drinking and revelry. On January 25th, Robert Burns' birthday is celebrated world-wide and the traditional ceremony is in line with what he loved, poetry, song, haggis, and whisky.

Situational Drinking:

Scotch is a drink for all occasions, before dinner, after dinner, before head-butting someone who has cast aspersions on you, after head-butting someone who has cast aspersions on you.

Here are a few situations where a dram or two of scotch will work perfectly and the specific scotch you should drink in that given situation.

Before Dinner: Auchentoshan Three Word: Aged in American bourbon, Jerez Sherry, and Port wood, this stunner is light bodied, with a nutty softness and notes of orange peel and spice. Before dinner you don't want richness, you want something that is going to wake up you palette and get your brain into the mood for food. Auchentoshan shows up on this blog pretty regularly for a reason, it is reasonably price, it's easy to drink and just tasty as hell.

After Dinner: The Macallan 12: A rich, heavy scotch aged in Jerez Sherry barrels with notes of dried fruit, vanilla, and spice. This scotch is still lively and lives up in the palette but it doesn't burn the mouth. After dinner you want some sweetness and richness in your whisky. The Macallan does the trick nicely by pairing with dark chocolate, creme brûlée and dried fruits.

With a Cigar: Bruichladdie 1990 Spirit Cask Range Cognac Cask: The name isn't the only mouthful. Bruichladdie has been long loved/detested for their never ended range of different ages and finishes*** on their beautifully soft and easy drinking whisky. This particular one spends 18 years in cognac barrels which allows the spirit to take on amazing grapey qualities as well as rich notes of mint and spice. All of these factors make it go amazingly with a great cigar. I am not a big cigar guy, but if I could afford to drink the 1990 Cognac you better believe I would become one.

After Shoveling Your Driveway: Ardbeg Uigedail: This fifteen year old Islay Whiskey matches powerful smokey peat flavours, with a deep backbone of briny sea water and a rich sherry sweetness. At 54% this whisky will warm you up from the deepest freeze. There is nothing like coming inside from a few hours of shoveling to have a few fingers of this beautiful whisky to warm you from the inside out.

Before Bed: Bowmore 18: This is a classic Islay that actually does a bit of an about face from the Ardbeg. Bowmore 18 is a sweet whiskey with beautiful notes of Dutch chocolate, plum and other dried fruit. Aged for 18 years in sherry barrels this whisky has a voluptuously creamy mouthfeel and just enough heat to make you want to curl up in bed. From someone who has some trouble turning off my brain before bed, Bowmore 18 would be a great way to drift off.

*Think New Years Eve.

**I swear I have been told this by multiple people, over the years, that they love him for his Scottishness. Not my word, but I will steal it.

***In the store, where I worked, I kept somewhere between 46 and 60 different Bruichladdich SKUs in stock at all times.

Recipe: Pappardelle w/ Portobello Garlic Butter Sauce

*Now that the militant vegetarians are gone I am going to talk shit about them. What many vegetarians in North America don't know is that most of the people who live in the 3rd world do live a vegetarian lifestyle, but it's not by choice. Animal protein is a life giving luxury, that must be purchased, hunted, or scrounged at great cost or effort. Butter and cheese are two animal products that would be coveted in the 3rd world. They are more stable and easy to transport forms of animal protein. So in other words, most of the world's vegetarians are not happy about it. Just keep it in mind when you chide someone for enjoying meat.

As I promised in yesterday's article I will be doing some vegetarian recipes to help those of you who have decided to do Meatless Mondays. Now there is a section of the vegetarian community who would abhor the use of butter or cheese in this dish. If you are those people find the little arrow on your browser which points to your left and kindly leave the page.*

Vegetarian Cuisine gets a bad reputation for being boring or lacking in flavour. When it comes to veggie burgers and rice dishes I would tend to agree. But when you start to dig into some more ethnic cuisine meat is not necessary for amazing flavour. This dish is super simple but also amazingly rewarding.

Ingredients: 2 servings Pappardelle

2 Portobello mushrooms (washed, 1/2 chop)

2 cloves Garlic (finely chopped0

1 Red onion

1/3 stick Butter

Grape seed oil

Parmigiano Reggiano

4 Sage leaves

Directions:

Set a pot of water to boil. In a sauce on medium heat add grape seed oil. Add the onions and sweat them until translucent. Add the garlic and continue to cook down the onions which will begin to brown. Then add the portobello. Sauté the contents of the pan until the mushroom has turned a dark brown and the onions begin to caramelize. Then add the butter which should deglaze the pan while it melts stir vigorously. And grate some Parmigiano Reggiano into the pan and continue to sauté. When the pasta is done to al dente add the pasta to the sauce pan along with a small amount of the pasta water. Allow the contents of the sauce pan to cook all together for about two minutes, salt and pepper to taste and then plate with more parmigiano reggiano on top. Garnish with sage leaves. The aromatics of the sage will add to the earthiness of the mushroom and the sweetness of the onion.

Recipe: Pan Roasted Duck Breast w/ Blueberry Gastrique & Mushroom Crostini

Since I started doing recipes on Braised Blue, I have done my best to really keep things simple and explanatory. Today's Recipe is the hardest one I've ever posted as it brings together a number of different components, ingredients and techniques. The flavour profile is a play on a few classic French duck dishes by pairing the duck with a sweet and sour element and also an earthy element. With this in mind, it's also one of the best things I've ever made, and though it seems like a lot. It actually only took me about an hour and 15 minutes from start to finish.

Duck is an amazing ingredient. It's rich, it's flavourful, and it's actually pretty healthy if prepared properly. Duck is also a really difficult ingredient to work with because it is unforgiving, fatty and cooking it takes a lot of patience and timing. If you were so inclined with this dish you could substitute venison, elk, or even a nice beer tenderloin and the flavours would still work together. But there is one great thing with working with duck….Duck Fat. Duck fat is the richest, darkest, and most aromatic substances known to man. When you make duck breasts you get a lot of duck fat that you can save and use in your cooking for the next few months. Bacon drippings get the hell out of the way, duck has entered the room.

Part 1. The Duck

Ingredients:

Duck breasts (the skin should remain on and should be deeply scored in a checker board pattern)

Sea salt

Cinnamon

Cayenne pepper

Directions: Preheat oven to 350. Make sure to score the skin of the duck in a checker board pattern this will allow the thick layer of fat which resides beneath the skin to render more quickly. It will also allow the skin to crisp much better. Use the salt, cinnamon, and cayenne to coat both sides of the duck. In a very hot cast iron skillet the breasts should be placed skin down. The pan needs to be screaming hot to really crisp the skin and render the fat. Don't be afraid there is enough fat there so that it shouldn't burn. The rendering should take about four to six minutes. Once the skin is crispy and the breasts have released their fat. Turn the breasts and sear the skinless side. This should take about two minutes.*

*It is very important to always flip away from you there will be quite a bit of fat that will have collected by now and if it was to splash while you flipped the meat. The splash should not be towards yourself. I've learned and relearned this rule in the past and I would recommend not learning it for yourself.

Then remove the duck from the pan and place on paper towels to rest. Pour off the duck fat into a container, and in the same cast iron skillet place the breasts back into the pan skin side up. Then place in the oven. The breasts should roast for about 8-10 minutes, I like my duck medium-rare but there is no shame in liking your poultry totally cooked through. After they roast remove the skillet and let the breasts rest for about five minutes.

Part 2: The Gastrique:

Ingredients: 1 cup Blueberries(fresh if possible)

Balsamic Vinegar

1 tsp Cinnamon

1 tsp Cayenne

1 tbs Butter

Sea salt

Black pepper

Directions: Place your blueberries in a sauce pan on medium/low heat. Add a tiny bit of water, the salt, pepper, cayenne, and cinnamon. Simmer these together until the berries begin to break down. Deglaze with the balsamic and then add enough to cover the berries. Reduce by half, add butter, simmer for about five minutes remove from heat and cover.

Part 3: The Crostini

Ingredients: 1.5 cups of Chanterelle mushrooms

Diced garlic

Duck fat

Salt

Pepper

French bread

Parmigiano Reggiano

Recipe Redux: This dish works on a bunch of different levels of flavour. The Duck is rich, dense meat with a smokey, and slightly spicy crust on the skin. The gastrique is sweet and sour but with a really deep dark flavour. I would recommend 2009 Brancaia Tre. It's a blend of Sangiovese, Cabernet Sauvignon and Merlot from three different vineyards in Tuscany. There is light cherry notes with deeper dark berry notes in the mid to back palette really do well to soften the ample tannins with give a little bit of grip. The acidity of the wine is in balance but it is high which makes it really work well with food.

Directions:

Use your reserved duck fat in a pan on medium/low heat add your garlic and mushrooms. Sauté for about five minutes letting the mushrooms really absorb the duck fat. Then brush the hot duck fat onto your bread which should be ready on a baking sheet. Top the bread with the mushrooms and garlic. Liberally, microplane the parmigiano reggiano onto the mushrooms and bread. Place in oven on a high broil for about three minutes. The bread should crisp, the cheese should become one with the mushrooms. Remove from the oven and top with some course sea salt.

Part 4: Bringing it all together.

This should all be served as one dish along side a simple tomato, onion and cucumber salad with a simple vinaigrette. The gastric and macerated blueberries should be used to top your duck. The crostini should be eaten with the dish as well**. And it should all really just work in harmony together. Try your best to get the blue berries into every bite of duck as it really cuts through the richness of the meat with nice acid, spice and sweetness. Enjoy!

**As you eat try combining the different flavours. You will see that everything really plays off everything else. The cinnamon and spice ties the duck to the blueberries. The duck fat in the mushrooms and bread connects it to the duck and the sweetness and tartness from the blueberries works with the deep earthiness from the mushrooms.